I0077018

RISK
MANAGEMENT
REVISITED

*How to Survive in the Age
of Misinformation*

Copyright © John P. Kindinger 2015
All rights reserved.

ISBN-10: 0692458417
ISBN-13: 978-0692458419

Library of Congress Control Number: 2015908820

Published by Kindinger Strategic Advisors, LLC
3130 Indian Trail
Eustis, Florida 32726

Cover Photo – **EMP Rise.** This image shows the detonation of the Starfish Prime nuclear device over the Pacific Ocean producing the first electromagnetic pulse (EMP) event on July 9, 1962. This was the view of the detonation as seen from about 900 miles away in Honolulu, Hawaii. Photo from the *Report of the Commission to Assess the Threat to the United States from Electromagnetic Pulse (EMP) Attack*, Volume 1: Executive Report, Graham, et al, 2004.

DEDICATION

To Cindy whose patience and support made this project possible.

TABLE OF CONTENTS

TABLE OF EXHIBITS

Preface

After having spent over thirty years learning quantitative risk assessment methods and applying them to a wide spectrum of hazardous activities and critical business decisions, I was considering the idea of writing a book recounting my experiences and, hopefully, providing some insights that would help others become productive risk managers without having to repeat all the lessons I had to learn the hard way. In addition, there were still many application areas where risk was not being assessed or managed at all well. I was ready to wail on ill-conceived and ineffective practices in fields like project management and business analytics where snake oil salesmen were getting rich promoting methods and tools that were one step above voodoo (no offense to voodoo devotees).

But recent events have caused me to step back and gasp at the colossal failures to manage risk that have occurred in systems where most people, including me, thought that safeguards were in place to prevent catastrophic events or at least significantly mitigate their impact on our lives. After experiencing the Great Recession, the Macondo oil spill, or the Tōhoku earthquake and resulting Fukushima nuclear disaster, how many people would accept the proposition that risk management really works and can be relied on to protect us from even man-made catastrophes let alone natural events? Not many.

So upon reflection, I decided that there was a much greater need for a book on risk management aimed at non-experts who are barraged daily by all manner of advice and promotions claiming to eliminate risk in their lives. Obviously much of this "advice" regarding risk is just self-serving salesmanship or even predatory misdirection. But in spite of all the conflicting claims, people still need to make decisions that will critically affect their personal lives and our greater collective welfare. This book is dedicated to advancing the abilities of the reader to navigate his or her own course through the wilderness of incomplete and confusing information to make rational, informed decisions on issues that impact their personal lives and the greater societal issues we face collectively.

Overview

So how do I go about accomplishing this ambitious goal of writing a book on risk management for the masses? First, I know this cannot be just a text book with a flashy cover. But, some important technical fundamentals will need to be comprehensively explained because, as we shall see, risk and risk management are not well understood concepts. I will, therefore, try to achieve a balance between the explanation of what risk is and how to assess and measure it with relevant examples of how failure to do this well can lead to disaster. In addition to dissecting catastrophes that have already happened, I'll try to look forward and provide what I hope you will find to be genuinely useful insights into what we individually and collectively should be worrying about in the future.

To start out I will look at three recent major catastrophes that have cost so much in lives and treasure and left us all wondering what could have been done to reduce the consequences or even prevent them from happening all together. After providing a brief synopsis of each event, I will examine the degree to which risk management was used (or not) prior to the event and the degree to which it failed in each case.

From the examination of these real world risk management failures, I'll make some comments about the level of professionalism that exists (or not) in the practice of risk analysis and risk management. This discussion leads to the unfortunate conclusion that competent and objective risk analysis is not widely practiced. As a result, we will need to take some time in Part II to describe the basic principles that need to be followed in performing good risk analysis and identify some of the proven methods available for doing it well.

After having established a foundation of understanding on risk management principles and methods, Part III will systematically examine the reasons why risk management can fail and provide a rich set of warning signs to look for when evaluating the risk management assurances made by others.

Finally in Part IV, I'll put the concepts and methods presented to the test and actually conduct an assessment of potential mega fatality risk events that I think you will find informative and maybe even a little frightening.

Part I – A Report Card on Risk Management

Chapter 1 - MACONDO - REVISITED

Synopsis of Event [1,2,3,4]

Macondo was an exploration well drilled in the Gulf of Mexico about 48 miles southeast of the mouth of the Mississippi River in an area with a water depth of approximately 5,000 feet. The project was primarily funded and planned by BP (formerly British Petroleum) Corporation using a semi-submersible mobile offshore drilling unit (MODU) contracted from Transocean Corporation. Unlike fixed drilling platforms used in shallower water, MODUs can move from one location to another under their own power. Dynamically positioned MODUs utilize satellite positioning technology connected to powerful directional thrusters to maintain themselves in place over a subsea wellhead.

The initial drilling of the Macondo well was begun in October 2009 by Transocean's semi-submersible *Marianas* and continued until November 2009 when *Marianas* had to be removed after being damaged by Hurricane Ida. At that time, the *Marianas* drilling had reached more than 9,000 feet below the ocean surface (4,000 feet below the seabed), with another 9,000 feet to go to the anticipated oil and gas reservoir. In February 2010 BP relocated Transocean's *Deepwater Horizon* rig to the Macondo site and resumed drilling. By April 20 2010, the well had been drilled to a depth of 18,360 feet and had successfully discovered oil in a hydrocarbon-bearing Miocene reservoir. At this point, the decision was made to temporarily abandon the Macondo well and complete it as a production well in the future.

At approximately 9:50 p.m. on the evening of April 20, 2010, while the crew of the *Deepwater Horizon* rig was finishing work after drilling the Macondo exploratory well, an undetected influx of hydrocarbons (commonly referred to as a "kick") escalated to a blowout. Shortly after the blowout, hydrocarbons that had flowed onto the rig floor through a mud-gas vent line ignited in two separate explosions. Flowing hydrocarbons fueled a fire on the rig that continued to burn until the rig sank on April 22. Eleven men died on the *Deepwater Horizon* that evening. Over the next 87 days, almost five million barrels of oil were discharged from the Macondo well into the Gulf of Mexico.

The five million barrels (210 million gallons) of crude oil discharged from the Macondo blowout produced the largest accidental marine oil spill in U.S. history. The immediate consequences are captured graphically in the picture on the next page taken from orbit by NASA showing the massive extent of the discharge plume. Longer term consequences to the Gulf ecosystem and the exposed human population will take years to fully understand.

Exhibit 1-1 NASA's Terra Satellite Sees the Macondo Blowout on May 24, 2010

To put the environmental significance of this event in perspective, the leakage from all previous ocean well accidents drilled in U.S. waters totaled to about 200,000 barrels. This figure includes the previous worst case accident, the Union Oil Company Platform A-21 blowout in the Santa Barbara Channel in 1969.

To cover costs of environmental restoration, compensation claims, and fines, BP has thus far set aside 43 *billion* dollars and their final total may exceed 60 billion dollars[5]. In addition, BP's partners in Macondo - Anadarko Petroleum, Halliburton, and Transocean are each potentially liable for billions more[6]. As an aside, this probably sets the world record for project cost overruns, at least outside of government.

Risk Assessment Performed

All of the investigations of the Macondo accident pointed out the rather obvious failure of BP to properly assess and manage risk. However, only the report prepared by the Bureau of Ocean Energy Management, Regulation, and Enforcement (BOEMRE) [3] (formerly the Minerals Management Service or "MMS") provided any real insight into what was actually done, or not, in this regard.

The following significant findings are taken from Section XV of the BOEMRE report:

- To assess risk, the BP Macondo engineering design team used a risk register, which was a spreadsheet that the team created to anticipate risks and to identify individuals assigned to mitigate risks.
- The risk categories available in the risk register include the following: health and safety, environmental, reputation, cost, schedule, production, reserves, and net present value. In the Macondo risk register, BP design personnel identified 23 risks that were placed into only three different categories – cost, production and schedule – and chose not to categorize any of them as "health and safety" risks. For example, BP personnel identified a well control problem as a "cost" and not a "health and safety" risk.
- BP personnel testified that a register or "ledger" was used throughout the process of drilling the well. BOEMRE investigators found that the Macondo team did not perform any risk analyses (or mitigation analyses) using the risk register after June 20, 2009 (drilling began in November 2009). Thus, the risk register was only utilized during the Macondo well design phase and not during BP's execution of day-to-day operations at the well.
- In addition, "the BOEMRE review found that in the weeks leading up to the blowout on April 20, the BP Macondo team made a series of operational decisions that reduced costs and increased risk. The BOEMRE review did not find any explicit statements by BP personnel that any of these decisions were made as part of a conscious cost/risk trade-off. However, the evidence the Panel reviewed suggests that the Macondo team made a series of decisions that cut costs and saved time. Moreover, the Panel found

no evidence that the cost-cutting and time-saving decisions were subjected to any formal risk assessment processes." [3]

Later in this book after I have laid out the basics of how risk assessment should be done, we will refer back to these findings and discuss how the Macondo risk assessment could have been done successfully. Until then, I will leave you with the following brief comments on the BOEMRE findings.

- A "risk register" is a simplistic, qualitative (high, medium, low) risk assessment tool totally inadequate for assessing the risk of complex, low frequency, high consequence events, like the Macondo blowout. The real focus of the risk register was project cost and schedule risk, which it isn't much good for either, but that is another story.

- There was no systematic risk management process in place at BP for Macondo. The risk register, pathetic as it was, was obviously done during the design phase of the project only to "punch a ticket" and obtain the required MMS permits. It was then totally ignored and not used in any way to monitor actual risk during drilling operations.

Risk Reduction Actions Taken

From the previous section one might conclude that BP had no concern what so ever for the risk of a blowout at Macondo. But let's step back for a moment and ask why they might have been so oblivious to the risks they faced.

Macondo was not the first offshore oil well to suffer a blowout. In the early years of shallow water offshore drilling, three very significant accidents preceded Macondo. They were:

Date	Event	Consequences
January 28, 1969	Union Oil Company Platform A-21 in the Santa Barbara Channel	80,000 to 100,000 barrels of oil released producing an 800-square-mile slick of oil that blackened an estimated 30 miles of California beaches
February 10, 1970	Chevron's Platform C in the Gulf of Mexico off Louisiana	65,000 barrels of crude oil released
December 1, 1970	Shell Platform B in the Bay of Marchand. Gulf of Mexico	Four fatalities, 36 injuries, 53,000 barrels of crude oil released

These accidents, of course, gathered considerable negative public attention. The U.S. government response included a moratorium on all drilling and production in California waters, a great increase in the regulation and oversight of offshore drilling by the Interior Department including the creation of the Minerals Management Service (MMS), and even the impetus for passage of the National Environmental Policy Act (NEPA). Macondo was operating under approvals from the MMS for existing regulations at the time of the accident. That said, a final judgment on this statement may not be in for some time.

The main point from a risk perspective, however, is that the BP Macondo team no doubt believed that they were compliant with comprehensive regulations that had worked to prevent large scale blowouts for 30 years. The exhibit below appears prominently in the report of the internal BP accident investigation.[4]

Exhibit 1-2 Barriers Breached and the Relationship of Barriers to Critical Factors

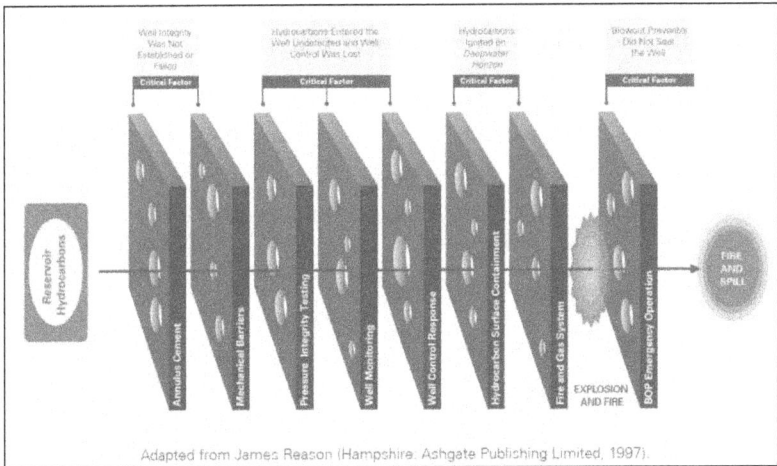

Adapted from James Reason (Hampshire: Ashgate Publishing Limited, 1997).

Source: Reference 4, p32.

The BP description for this exhibit is "Barriers Breached ---". I believe the impression they hoped to create is that the accident required the unfortunate alignment of all the "critical factors" shown and, as a result, was very complex and very difficult, if not impossible, to anticipate. From published reports, I especially got the impression that they believed the final barrier, the blowout preventer (BOP) made them bulletproof[7]. That is, in making decisions regarding well control, the worst that could possibly happen is that the BOP would actuate to seal a bad well that was going to be abandoned temporarily in any case. As it turned out, this confidence was sadly misplaced. The BOP appears to have been defeated by a disturbingly simple failure scenario. The "shear ram" that was the last line of defense in the BOP required the *Deepwater Horizon's* dynamic positioning system to hold the 5,000 foot long drillpipe in

11

position above the BOP and centered in the jaws of the shear ram. During the blowout and explosions on the *Deepwater Horizon*, the drillpipe could no longer be maintained in its proper position and the drillpipe moved enough to prevent the shear ram from sealing the well when it was actuated. The next exhibit presents an illustration of how the shear ram was supposed to work (left side sequence) and how it failed (right side sequence) at Macondo.

Exhibit 1-3 Blowout Preventer Failure[8]

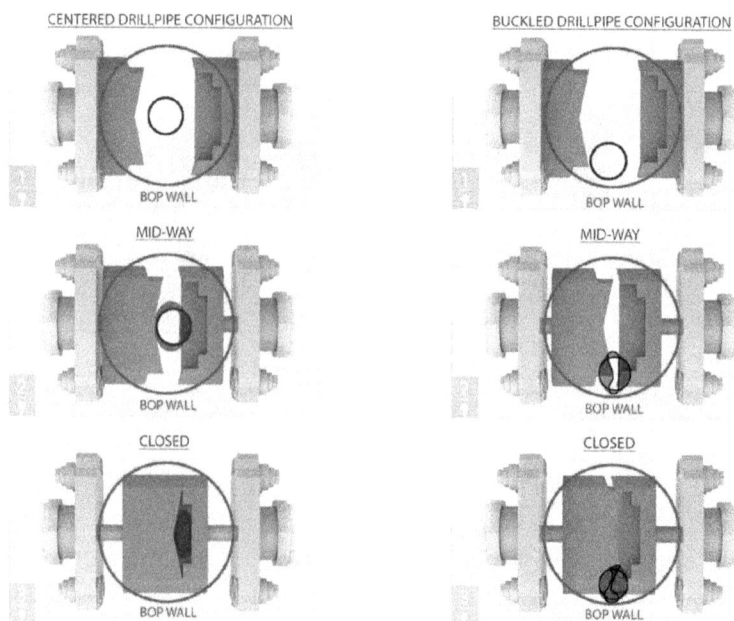

The BOP failure is an example of a multiple failure accident scenario. That is it did take the occurrence of several events to make the failure happen. If all the possible scenarios that could cause such a failure were considered, the number of such scenarios would have quickly overwhelmed the capabilities of the risk register spreadsheet. Later we will discuss risk analysis methods and tools that can easily handle this type of problem. This higher level of analysis was not (and as far as I can tell, is not) required by regulations and was not deemed necessary by BP.

Grade Summary

To summarize how risk management failed to prevent the Macondo blowout or any of the events we will examine, I will cast what we know into answers to the four questions listed in the table below. For the unwanted event to have happened, the answer to at least one of the questions must be NO.

How Did Risk Management Fail?	Answer?	Comments
Was blowout risk assessed for Macondo?	NO	Blowout risk was considered in regulations requiring a BOP, but no Macondo specific assessment of blowout risk was done.
Did the risk analysis identify blowout as important?	NO	Not applicable, no specific assessment of blowout risk was done for Macondo.
Were risk reduction actions taken to reduce likelihood and/or consequences?	YES	Regulations required a blowout preventer (BOP) to be installed on Macondo.
Did implemented risk reduction actions work to prevent the event and/or mitigate the consequences?	NO	The BOP required by regulation was failed by a scenario that could have been identified by risk analysis.

---

[1] Deep Water, The Gulf Oil Disaster and the Future of Offshore Drilling, Report to the President, National Commission on the BP Deepwater Horizon Oil Spill and Offshore Drilling, January 2011.
[2] Macondo, The Gulf Oil Disaster, Chief Council's Report, National Commission on the BP Deepwater Horizon Oil Spill and Offshore Drilling, 2011.

[3] Report Regarding the Causes of the April 20,2010 Macondo Oil Well Blowout, The Bureau of Ocean Energy Management, September 14, 2011.

[4] Deepwater Horizon Accident Investigation Report, BP Corporation, September 8, 2010.

[5] Judge Hammers BP for Gulf Disaster, Daniel Gilbert & Justin Scheck, *The Wall Street Journal,* 9/5/2014.

[6] Halliburton Agrees to Pay $1.1 Billion for Gulf Spill, Daniel Gilbert, *The Wall Street Journal,* 9/3/2014.

[7] On Doomed Rig's Last day, A Decisive change of Plan, Russell Gold & Ben Casselman, *The Wall Street Journal*, 8/26/10.

[8] Explosion And Fire At The Macondo Well, Investigation Report Volume 2, page 43, U.S. Chemical Safety and Hazard Investigation Board, 6/5/2014

Chapter 2 - THE GREAT RECESSION - FAILURE IN PROGRESS

Synopsis of Event

The following excerpt from the Preface of the official report of the Financial Crisis Inquiry Commission (FCIC) sums up the impacts of this event on the U. S. economy and society.

The profound events of 2007 and 2008 were neither bumps in the road nor an accentuated dip in the financial and business cycles we have come to expect in a free market economic system. This was a fundamental disruption --a financial upheaval, if you will -- that wreaked havoc in communities and neighborhoods across this country.

As this report goes to print (January 2011), there are more than 36 million Americans who are out of work, cannot find full-time work, or have given up looking for work. About four million families have lost their homes to foreclosure and another four and a half million have slipped into the foreclosure process or are seriously behind on their mortgage payments. Nearly $11 trillion in household wealth has vanished, with retirement accounts and life savings swept away. Businesses, large and small, have felt the sting of a deep recession. There is much anger about what has transpired, and justifiably so. Many people who abided by all the rules now find themselves out of work and uncertain about their future prospects. The collateral damage of this crisis has been real people and real communities. The impacts of this crisis are likely to be felt for a generation. And the nation faces no easy path to renewed economic strength.

And, as of this writing in 2015, the effects of Great Recession are still being felt by many. Although the overall economy, as measured by GDP, has recovered from the Great Recession by the end of 2011, many other metrics remain depressed. The next two graphs show that recovery in the GDP has not been realized by the average family.

Exhibit 2-1 Real U.S. Median Household Income

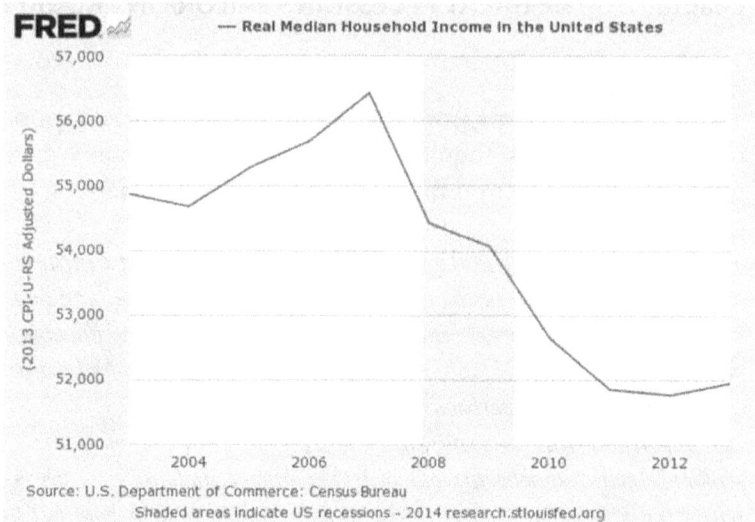

FRED — Real Median Household Income in the United States

Source: U.S. Department of Commerce: Census Bureau
Shaded areas indicate US recessions - 2014 research.stlouisfed.org

Exhibit 2-2 U.S. National Income Expectations

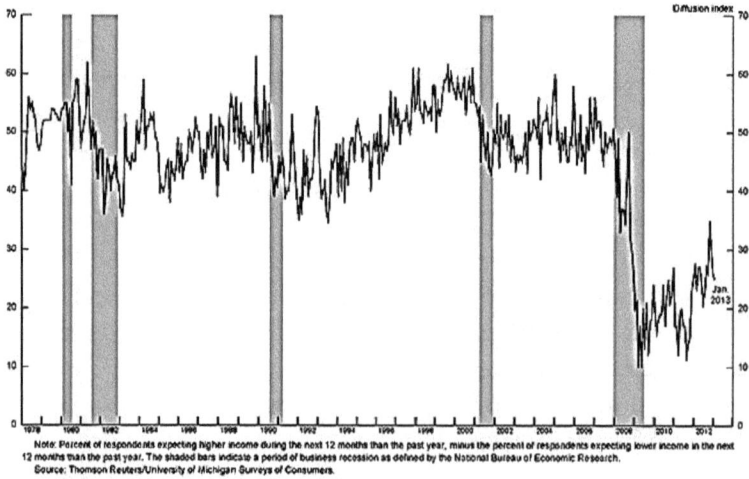

Exhibit 5: Nominal Income Expectations

Note: Percent of respondents expecting higher income during the next 12 months than the past year, minus the percent of respondents expecting lower income in the next 12 months than the past year. The shaded bars indicate a period of business recession as defined by the National Bureau of Economic Research.
Source: Thomson Reuters/University of Michigan Surveys of Consumers.

So how did this debacle happen and how could it have been prevented? The FCIC lists many causes but delivers no clear answer. The official report conclusions lay primary blame on corporate excesses and inadequate regulation and call for more

16

financial regulation and greater government oversight of just about everything. But four of the ten commissioners dissented (along partisan lines) from these recommendations and offered separate conclusions that largely blamed misguided government policies for the debacle.

So what is a risk analyst who is not a PhD economist to make of this situation? Here's my simple minded and very brief assessment of what the FCIC report really says.

1. The fundamental cause of the Great Recession was the enormous bubble in U.S. housing values made possible by the proliferation of government promoted sub-prime mortgages requiring little or no down payment. Exhibits 2-3 and 2-4 show the magnitude of the price bubble and the corresponding explosion in sub-prime mortgages.

2. Next, a downturn in home prices very quickly caused the value of many homes to fall below their outstanding loan balance. This combined with an increase in unemployment caused many home owners to default on these sub-prime loans. Exhibit 2-5 shows this dramatic rise in mortgage delinquencies.

3. The resulting tsunami of mortgage loan losses then overwhelmed all safeguards meant to protect the integrity of the financial system. It is my belief that all the many other "causes" discussed in the FCIC report were actually symptoms of the stress placed on the overall financial system by this load of bad debt.

Exhibit 2-3 The Home Price Bubble

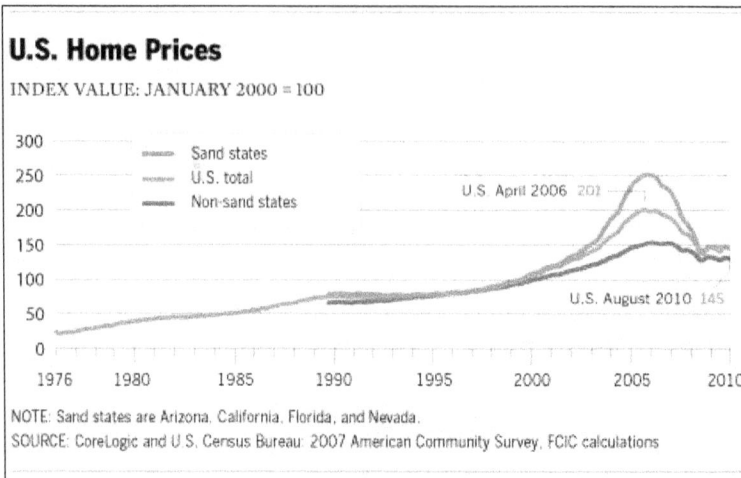

U.S. Home Prices

INDEX VALUE: JANUARY 2000 = 100

NOTE: Sand states are Arizona, California, Florida, and Nevada.
SOURCE: CoreLogic and U.S. Census Bureau: 2007 American Community Survey, FCIC calculations

From FCIC Report, Figure 6.2

Exhibit 2-4 The Explosion of No Down Payment Mortgages

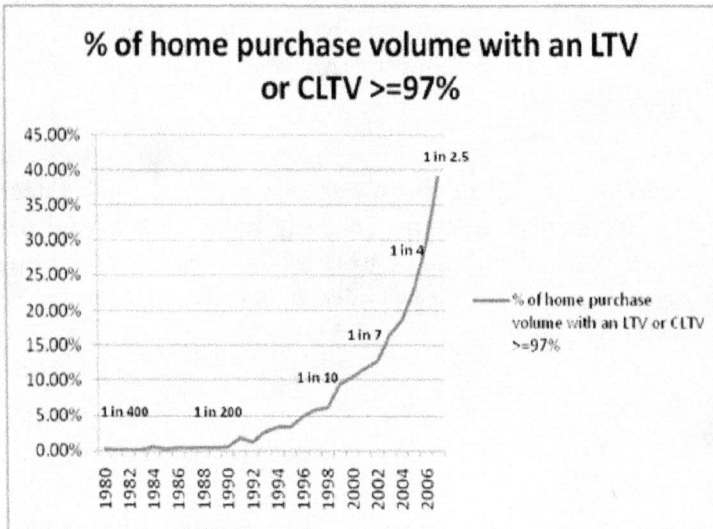

% of home purchase volume with an LTV or CLTV >=97%

From FCIC Report, page 494
Sources: FHA 2009 Actuarial Study, and HUD"s Office of Policy Development and Research – Profiles of GSE Mortgage Purchases in 1999 and 2000, in 2001-2004, and in 2005-2007, and Fannie's 2007 10-K.
Compiled by Edward Pinto   LTV = loan to value

Exhibit 2-5 The Default Tsunami

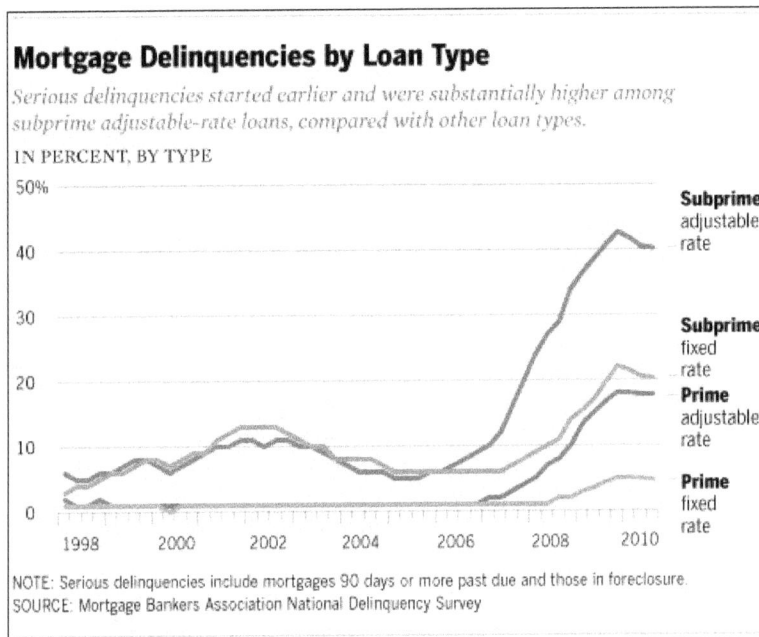

Mortgage Delinquencies by Loan Type

Serious delinquencies started earlier and were substantially higher among subprime adjustable-rate loans, compared with other loan types.

IN PERCENT, BY TYPE

NOTE: Serious delinquencies include mortgages 90 days or more past due and those in foreclosure.
SOURCE: Mortgage Bankers Association National Delinquency Survey

From FCIC Report, Figure 11.2

Risk Assessment Performed

The words "risk" and "risk management" can be found on almost every page of the FCIC report including many times in the official conclusions of both the main report and the dissents.   There is a consistent context in which risk management is mentioned, *failure*.   But in its 662 pages, the report never comprehensively addresses the subject head on. Risk and risk management are never defined and remarkably little insight is given into how risk management failed. Was risk assessed?   Did the risk assessments fail to quantify potential losses?   Did managers fail to enact prudent risk mitigation strategies? Did these strategies fail? I have to conclude that the repeated identification of risk management failure in this report is a palliative, not a rigorous finding.   A much more serious review of financial risk management practices is needed than can be found in this report.

That said, the points below provide a summary of what I was able to glean from the FCIC regarding risk assessment.

- Most if not all players in the financial system were using some level of quantitative analysis to predict the potential benefits and risks of their investments. One widely used method was the "Value at Risk" (VaR) model first developed by JP Morgan. These models supposedly are able to predict with at least 95% certainty how much a firm could lose if market prices changed.

- Using tools like VaR analysis, financial institutions created new highly leveraged securities such as credit default swaps (CDS), collateralized debt obligations (CDO) and synthetic CDO's to finance mortgages. One witness told the FCIC that "Wall Street is essentially floating on a sea of mathematics and computer power."

- The results from these models were undermined by the inexplicable use, apparently by an entire industry, of the following optimistic assumptions:
  o The assumption that housing prices would never decline significantly.
  o The assumption that housing prices were largely uncorrelated across different regions, so that a local housing bubble bursting in Nevada would not happen at the same time as one bursting in Florida.
  o The assumption that deliberate defaults by homeowners who could make their mortgage payments but chose not to would never be significant.
  o The assumption that markets for exotic financial products would always be liquid.

Together, these findings present a clear picture that risk analysis was being used to justify extreme risk taking rather than to inform prudent risk management. When housing prices declined nationally and quite severely in certain areas, these flawed assumptions, magnified by other problems described in the next paragraph, created catastrophic financial losses for firms exposed to housing investments.

Risk Reduction Actions Taken

The FCIC report is replete with quotes from high level financial officials pleading that "we were hedged", meaning that they thought that large risks were transferred to others through one of several hedging strategies. In addition to the risk assessment deficiencies listed above, these strategies failed because the potential consequences of mortgage losses on the overall financial system were also not known, or ignored. Some of these systemic risk problems discussed in the FCIC Report include:

- **Insufficient capital.** Some of the failed institutions were levered 35 to 1 or higher. This meant that every 35$ of assets was financed with 1$ of equity capital and 34$ of debt. This made these firms enormously profitable when things were going well, but incredibly sensitive to even a small loss, as a 3 percent decline in the market value of these assets would leave them technically insolvent. In some cases, this increased leverage was direct and transparent. In other cases, firms used Structured Investment Vehicles, asset-backed commercial paper conduits, and other off-balance-sheet entities to try to have it both ways: further increasing their leverage while appearing not to do so. Highly concentrated, highly correlated risk combined with high leverage makes a fragile financial sector and creates a financial accident waiting to happen. These firms should have had much larger capital cushions and/or mechanisms for contingent capital upon which to draw in a crisis.

- **Overdependence on short-term liquidity from repurchase agreements and commercial paper markets.** Just as each lacked sufficient capital cushions, in each case the failing firm's liquidity cushion ran out within days. The failed firms appear to have based their liquidity strategies on the flawed assumption that both the firm and these funding markets would always be healthy and functioning smoothly. By failing to provide sufficiently for disruptions in their short-term financing, management put their firm's survival on a hair trigger.

- **Poor risk integration systems.** A number of firms were unable to easily aggregate their housing risks across various business lines. Once the market began to decline, those firms that understood their total exposure were able to effectively sell or hedge their risk before the market turned down too far. Those that didn't were stuck with toxic assets in a disintegrating market.

Grade Summary

The preceding discussion of the Great Recession is largely taken from the subject matter experts who authored the FCIC report. But this humble risk analyst, who is not a PhD economist, would like to conclude with a few points that I think the report should say but does not.

First, the U.S. and international financial systems are sufficiently complex and interdependent that understanding their dynamic behavior is very difficult. In fact, the overall global financial system has demonstrated that it is dynamically unstable, that is, capable of non-linear behavior (causes and effects that are not proportional to each other) and sudden regime changes. The great recession plus the earlier Long Term Capital, Savings & Loan, and dot com crises illustrate that this has been the case for some time and that no one understands the dynamic behavior of the overall financial system well enough to be able to predict performance and quantify the risk (frequency or magnitude) of severe breakdowns or specify effective safeguards. This state of ignorance regarding the coming Great Recession was clearly demonstrated by none other than Federal Reserve Bank Chairman Ben Bernanke when in March 2006 he said, "I think we are unlikely to see growth being derailed by the housing market"[1] This condition of ignorance is the physical equivalent of walking one of the mesa tops in Los Alamos, New Mexico, where I once lived –at night. As long as you stay on the flat mesa top, you're good, but take one step over the shear edge of the mesa and the walk ends very badly.

Second, I believe that the global financial system will continue to grow even more complex and interdependent. As this happens, the dynamics will become even more difficult to comprehend and the risk of additional severe breakdowns is increasingly likely. To return to the mesa walk analogy, the cliff edge will become more jagged and the night darker.

A third point is that controlling risk by increasing the complexity of government regulation is likely to be unsuccessful in preventing future breakdowns. Regulatory changes always focus on preventing a recurrence of the last crisis while market participants move on and create new hazards. Plus, regulators are even more fragmented and myopic than the markets and institutions they oversee. This limits their ability to institute effective safeguards, even if they were able to model and anticipate future risks, an ability which they have not demonstrated thus far.

But please don't fall into despair and throw this book down because of this problem. Many people live on the mesas in Los Alamos without falling off the cliff edge. And there are other more complex systems we have learned to manage that are also capable of unstable behavior. A good example is the U.S. electric power system. The electric grid is a very complex and highly interdependent dynamic system. But like a wild beast, it is capable of spectacular and sudden bad behavior. Large blackouts don't happen very often, however, and there has never been a complete continent wide blackout. This is because of the great effort that has been made to tame the beast. System metrics that indicate the stability of the system are continuously monitored and automatic controls act to keep these parameters away from cliff edge values where they could become unstable. But occasionally complex multiple failures are able to breach these defenses and allow an outage to spread throughout large portions of the overall system. Sound familiar? To limit the risk of large blackouts, electric system operators fall back to very simple principles during times of great system stress. They deliberately sacrifice a compromised area of the grid to preserve the integrity of the larger system. This might sound draconian when applied to the financial system but what it could do is stop panic market overreactions and allow the damaged portion of the system to be restored after the offending problems have been identified and addressed.

In closing, I have again summarized how risk management failed to prevent the Great Recession into answers to the four questions listed in the table below. For the unwanted event to have happened, the answer to at least one of the questions must be NO.

How Did Risk Management Fail?	Answer?	Comments
Was broad financial system failure risk assessed by the mortgage industry?	NO	Risks of loss for individual securities were elaborately assessed but systemic failure was assumed to be impossible.
Did the risk analysis identify financial system failure as important?	NO	Systemic risk was assumed away by all participants.
Were risk reduction actions taken to reduce likelihood and/or consequences?	YES, sort of	Hedging strategies were thought to protect investors against all large losses.
Did implemented risk reduction actions work to prevent the event and/or mitigate the consequences?	NO	Hedging strategies failed when counterparties were unable to meet obligations.

---

[1] Little Alarm Shown at Fed At Dawn of Housing Bust, Jon Hilsenrath, Luca Di Leo, and Michael S Derby, *The Wall Street Journal*, 1/13/2012.

Chapter 3 - TŌHOKU – FUKUSHIMA & MOTHER NATURE

Synopsis of Event

The dramatic losses of life and property caused by recent natural events such as the Thailand earthquake and tsunami of 2004, Hurricane Katrina (2005), the Haiti earthquake in 2009, the New Zealand earthquakes of 2010 and 2011, and most recently the Tōhoku earthquake and tsunami in Japan merit examination in any discussion of risk. So let's take a closer look at earthquake risk in general and in particular, the Tōhoku earthquake and the resulting disaster at the Fukushima Daiichi nuclear power plant

The next exhibit graphs both the number of earthquakes greater than magnitude 7.0 and the estimated number of deaths resulting from earthquakes over the last thirty years. Without performing any statistical analysis on the data, two inferences can be made. First, the frequency of large earthquakes seems pretty steady. This is not surprising and if there was any evidence of changing seismic event frequencies, the professional seismology community would be on top of the story[1]. The number of deaths produced by these quakes, however, does not seem so well behaved. Several of the most deadly quakes in modern times have occurred in the last six years. Will future experience show that the first decade of the 21st century was just an outlier for earthquake fatalities or are we seeing the development of a trend? We don't know, but we can take a closer look at the question through the perspective of risk management.

Exhibit 3-1 Major Earthquakes and Resulting Fatalities

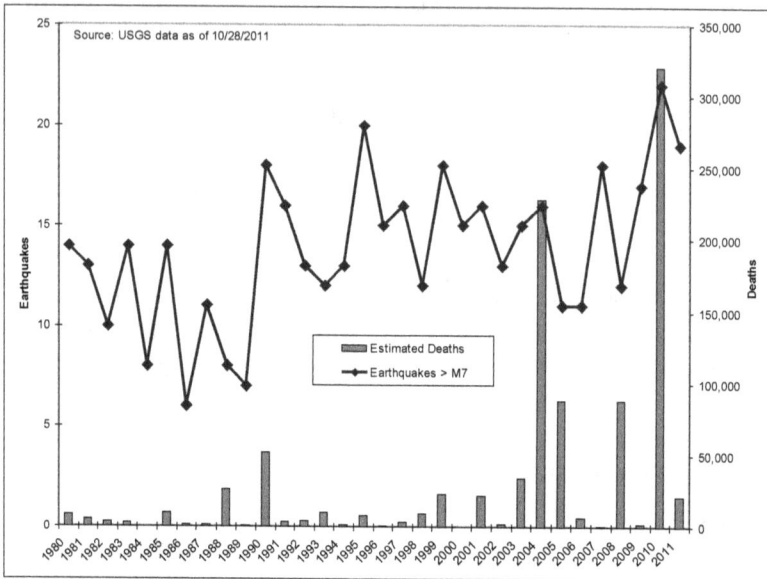

Earthquakes are, of course, acts of God or nature. Seismology can help us understand the statistical frequency and magnitude of future earthquakes expected in various locations but not the actual time of their occurrence. This means that seismic risk analysis can predict the statistical likelihood of earthquakes and the extent of damage suffered by structures, given the quake occurs. This is very useful for designing structures to better withstand earthquake forces and making emergency plans for responding to quakes quickly and effectively when they occur. So, overall, how good a job of seismic risk management are we doing? I think Exhibit 3-1 gives us cause to worry. Even in the United States where arguably the greatest efforts have been made in seismic risk analysis, we know that great quakes are statistically overdue on the deadly San Andreas and New Madrid faults. And when they do happen, even with the preparations that have been made, the resulting damage and loss of life could be devastating. In many other parts of the world little if any investment is made to reduce seismic risk and, as a result, even relatively low magnitude quakes can cause enormous damage when they strike in an unfortunate location.

With the human population steadily growing and growing fastest in less developed regions where seismic risk prevention is not a priority, earthquake fatalities may continue to rise.

We will return to the general question of earthquake risk later. But for this initial report card let's take a closer look at the role risk management played in the Tōhoku – Fukushima event.

On March 11, 2011 at about 2:46 P.M. local Japanese time, a magnitude 9.0 earthquake occurred about 70 kilometers (43 mi) east of the Tōhoku region of Honshu Island in the Pacific Ocean. The earthquake was centered in the subduction zone between the Pacific and North American tectonic plates and was one of the most powerful quakes ever recorded. Ground motion from the Tōhoku earthquake lasted about six minutes and moved portions of northeastern Japan by as much as 2.4 m (7.9 feet) closer to North America. This redistribution of planetary mass also caused a small shift in the Earth's axis increasing the speed of the Earth's rotation and shortening the length of a day by 1.8 microseconds.[2]

But it was the local effects of the quake in Japan that were most devastating. The ground motion throughout the Tōhoku region was intense with a maximum ground acceleration recorded at 2.93 gravities(g)[3]. The up thrust of the ocean floor also unleashed a massive tsunami wave that hit the coast at heights of as much as 29.6 meters (97 feet) and penetrated up to 10 km (6 miles) inland.[2,3] The combined forces of the earthquake and tsunami destroyed or damaged over 330,000 buildings, 2,100 roads, 56 bridges, and 26 railways. Most significantly, 20,350 people were killed or are missing and 130,000 were made homeless. The total economic loss in Japan is estimated at over 300 billion US dollars.[3]

In addition to the direct effects of the Tōhoku earthquake and tsunami that were experienced on March 11, this event was dramatically complicated by the damage that was incurred at the Fukushima Daiichi Nuclear Power Plant. Fukushima Daiichi is a six unit nuclear power station located on the coast about 150 km southwest of the earthquake epicenter. When the initial Tōhoku earthquake occurred, it produced ground motion measured at the plant about 25% greater than the values used for the plant design. Although a full assessment of initial damage may never be completely known, it appears that the inherent conservatism in the seismic design of the plant was sufficient to allow it to survive the much larger than design basis earthquake quite well. This was evidenced by the successful shutdown of the three operating reactors and successful starting and loading of emergency diesel generators in all six units.

About one hour after the initial earthquake, a tsunami wave about 15 meters (50 feet) high hit the plant and overwhelmed the 5.7 m (19 feet) seawall protecting units 1-4. The tsunami wave knocked out all the diesel generators located in the unprotected turbine buildings of units 1-4 and the metal enclosed switchgear that routed all electric power to the reactor buildings. Units 5 and 6 were newer and better protected from tsunamis and, were not operating at the time of the accident.

Exhibit 3-2 Tsunami Wave Striking Fukushima Daiichi

Source: The Tokyo Electric Power Co., Inc. Online Release: http://www.tepco.co.jp/tepconews/pressroom/110311/index-j.html

All the reactors at Fukushima Daiichi were boiling water reactors (BWRs) designed by the General Electric Co. These reactors require cooling water to be pumped into the core after shutdown to remove the residual decay heat that is generated from the nuclear fuel rods after shutdown. Without electric power, no water could be pumped into the cores of units 1-3 that had been operating. The water remaining in the core and in an external suppression pool will provide a few hours time margin to begin cooling water injection before core damage starts for this type of reactor. But with all units damaged at the same time and the surrounding area decimated, there was no hope of getting additional people or equipment to the plant quickly enough. Core damage began to occur before midnight on March 11.[4] The struggle to stop the damage, bring the reactors under full control and stem the release of radioactivity to the environment continues even now. Recent estimates for the cost of the plant cleanup plus compensation for affected residents exceed $105 billion.

Risk Assessment Performed

Seismic risk assessment requires the integration of two special disciplines. The first is seismology which strives to understand the geologic mechanisms that produce earthquakes and thereby predict their statistical frequency and magnitude. The second is structural engineering which uses the seismologists predicted ground motion for a specific site to design structures and systems capable of surviving the resulting stresses. Wow, you're thinking this must be complicated. Well, it can be, but in many cases the structural engineer just makes a conservative calculation of the maximum load (L) that a structure or system could see from the largest earthquake recorded in the subject area, and if the load (L) is less than the capacity (C) of the materials used in the structure, he will conclude that the structure is safe and that no further analysis is needed.

Complications arise, however, when the potential failure of the structure or system would be catastrophic and the difference between C and L are not great enough to allow uncertainties in these values to be ignored. The Exhibit below illustrates the problem graphically.

Exhibit 3-3 Seismic Risk Analysis Illustration

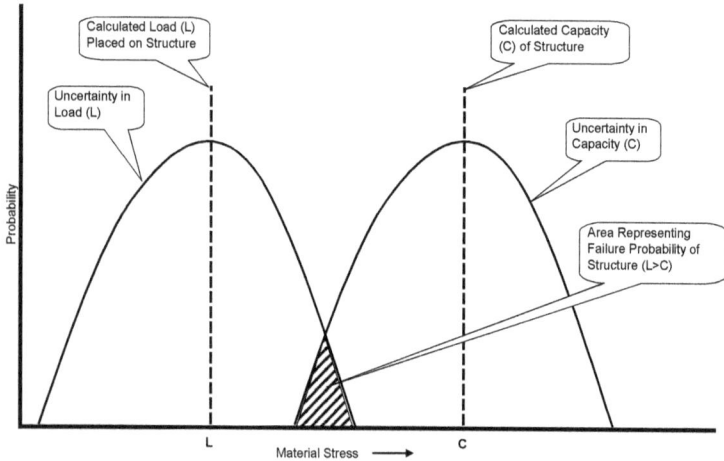

Although Japan is a very seismically active region, the largest earthquake observed in the century or so that accurate records have been kept was a Magnitude 8.5. Using the known history of earthquakes in the Fukushima region, the design basis earthquake (DBE) that was used to design and build the Fukushima Daiichi plants was set at about 0.45g[5] (the value for C). The actual ground acceleration measured on 3/11/2011 was 0.56g or about 25% greater than the DBE but, the plant did not fail from earthquake damage. This is because the uncertainty around the point value for C was not symmetrical as depicted in the simplified Exhibit above but heavily skewed to the right above the point value of C. In this case, the safety margin of extra capacity above the design point (C) was enough to save the hour, but not the day.

When the tsunami wave arrived an hour later, the result was different. In that case, the seawall height (C) was only about 19 feet while the wave height (L) was about 50 feet. No safety margin was available to save the plant. The remnants of the seawall can be seen in Exhibit 3-2 showing the tsunami wave coming ashore. The tsunami wave knocked out all the diesel generators located in the unprotected turbine buildings of units 1-4 and the metal enclosed switchgear that routed all electric power to the reactor buildings. Units 5 and 6 were newer and better protected from tsunamis and, were not operating at the time of the accident.

Independent reviews conducted after the accident[6] indicated that the plant owner, Tokyo Electric Power (Tepco), was aware of the lack of conservatism in the design of the seawall protecting units 1-4 and had not taken measures to improve the reliability of electric power supplies on site. This was later confirmed by Tepco when in October 2012, the company admitted that they understood the risk presented by a tsunami to the plant and ignored this risk out of fear that if admitted, the plant would have to be shut down. Recently, a judicial panel recommended that criminal charges be pursued against Tepco officers[7].

In the next sections we'll discuss this further.

Risk Reduction Actions Taken

In response to the frequent large earthquakes experienced in Japan, the government has established early warning systems for both large quakes and tsunamis. For earthquakes, the Japan Meteorological Agency (JMA) monitors more than 4,000 seismometers throughout Japan and issues an alert through TV, radio, and cell phone systems if a quake of greater than magnitude 5 is detected. For Tōhoku, the warning was issued about 31 seconds after the earthquake occurred which was about one minute before the earthquake was felt in Tokyo. It is believed that the early warning saved many lives.

Because of the size and location of the Tōhoku earthquake, the JMA also issued an immediate tsunami warning. But even with this warning, many thousands were unable to reach safe areas in time and lost their lives.

At the Fukushima Daiichi Nuclear Plants, extensive measures were taken in design and construction to enable the plant structures and systems to survive large quakes. As discussed above, these measures were successful even though Tōhoku produced much greater ground motion at the plant than was thought possible. Again as discussed above, the plants ability to withstand the accompanying tsunami was not sufficient. The story is not quite complete though because there was one additional feature of the plant design that was critical to the ultimate failure and needs further discussion.

In response to a review of seismic and tsunami risk done in the late 1990s, three additional backup electric generators capable of supplying any of the six reactors were installed in new buildings located at a higher elevation above the original plant. However, the metal clad switchgear through which the generators can be connected to the reactors critical cooling pumps was left unchanged in the lower, non-safety grade turbine buildings. All three of the generators added in the late 1990s were operational after the tsunami. If the metal clad switchgear had been moved to inside the reactor buildings or to other flood-proof locations, power would have been provided by these generators to the reactors' cooling systems and the core melt accidents avoided.[6]

Even though mentioned earlier, Tepco has admitted it knew of the tsunami risk faced by the plant and, failed to make corrective actions. Why they did a 90% fix for this issue by installing the additional emergency generators and not completing the job by upgrading or bypassing the vulnerable switchgear remains a mystery.

Grade Summary

Again, to summarize how risk management performed for the Tōhoku earthquake and tsunami, I have cast what we know into answers to the four questions listed in the table below. For the unwanted event to have happened, the answer to at least one of the questions must be NO.

How Did Risk Management Fail?	Answer?	Comments
Was risk assessed for Tōhoku the earthquake and tsunami?	YES	The high number of large earthquakes in Japan has focused the attention of the nation on earthquake and tsunami risk
Did the risk analysis identify Tōhoku type earthquakes and tsunamis as important?	YES	Even though the original design basis earthquake did not require protection for this large an event, reviews indicate that Tepco was aware of the risk from beyond design basis events.
Were risk reduction actions taken to reduce likelihood and/or consequences of these events?	NO, not sufficiently	In general, measures including rigorous building codes and early warning systems for both earthquakes and tsunami were effective and saved many lives. For Fukushima Daiichi, earthquake and tsunami protective features were included in the plant design, but only for a smaller magnitude event. Modifications that could have allowed the plant to withstand beyond design basis events were never installed.

How Did Risk Management Fail?	Answer?	Comments
Did implemented risk reduction actions work to prevent the event and/or mitigate the consequences?	NO, not sufficiently	In general, measures including rigorous building codes and early warning systems for both earthquakes and tsunami were effective and saved many lives. At Fukushima Daiichi, the plant survived the earthquake even though the design basis ground motion was exceeded. The tsunami, however, completely overwhelmed the protective seawall provided and destroyed critical plant electric power systems causing core damage in three reactors

Finally, in this Chapter I have attempted to capture the best available information about this disaster. But, I am sure new information will be forthcoming as investigations are completed and recovery accomplished. Even though it is now more than four years since the Fukushima Daiichi meltdowns, a comprehensive understanding of why earthquake and tsunami risk was so badly managed for this power plant has yet to emerge. Even though Tepco officials have now admitted their culpability in the inadequate plant design, just blaming current officials doesn't explain the bad decisions made over decades. Questions remaining to be answered include:

- Why wasn't evidence of the 869 AD earthquake and Tsunami used in setting the original design bases for the plant?

- How were units 1-4 allowed to continue operating without meaningful upgrades after units 5 & 6 were built to higher standards?
- Why were additional emergency generators installed without reliable connections to the units 1-4 emergency core cooling systems?

We may never know.

---

[1] Quakes Echo World-Wide, Gautam Naik, *The Wall Street Journal*, 3/28/2011.

[2] 2011 Tōhoku earthquake and tsunami. (2011, October 30). In *Wikipedia, The Free Encyclopedia*

[3] USGS earthquake summary,

[4] Fresh Tales of ChaosEmerge from Early inNuclear Crisis, Yuka Hayashi & Phred Dvorak, *The Wall Street Journal*, 5/18/2011, pA1

[5] Nuclear Power Plants and Earthquakes, World Nuclear Association, 9/2011

[6] Design Flaw Fueled Nuclear Disaster, Norihiko Shirouza & Chester Dawson, *The Wall Street Journal*, 7/1/2011

[7] Panel Says Ex-Tepco Execs Should Face Charges, Alexander Martin, *The Wall Street Journal*, 7/31/2014.

Chapter 4 - GRADING THE REPORT CARD

The tables below summarize the consequences produced by our three case study events and what we found about the role risk management played in their causation.

Exhibit 4-1 Report Card Event Consequences

	Event		
Consequences	Macondo Blowout	Great Recession	Tōhoku & Fukushima Daiichi Core Melts
Human Health	11 killed, 16 injured		20,350 people killed or missing and 130,000 made homeless
Estimated Monetary Loss/ Damages	$41 Billion	$11 Trillion	$300 Billion
Environmental & Other	210 million gallons of crude oil released into the Gulf of Mexico, significant ecosystem damage	Social and geopolitical changes may be significant and long lasting	Significant nuclear material contamination of environment

Exhibit 4-2 The Initial Report Card

How Did Risk Management Fail?			
Risk Management Questions	Macondo Blowout	Great Recession	Tōhoku & Fukushima Daiichi Core Melts
Was risk assessed for the event that actually happened?	NO	NO	YES
Did the risk analysis identify the actual event as important?	NO	NO	YES
Were risk reduction actions taken to reduce likelihood and/or consequences of the event?	YES	YES, sort of	NO, not sufficiently
Did implemented risk reduction actions work to prevent the event and/or mitigate its consequences?	NO	NO	NO, not sufficiently

But from the details of these events that we looked at come, I believe, some common threads that can help us all to do better in the future if we learn the right lessons from these disasters.

Ignoring or assuming away risk is dangerous – In all three of the cases examined the risk of the event that actually happened was somehow assumed to be impossible. The Macondo team never appears to have considered blowout risk in their decision making. Financial traders constructed elaborate hedging strategies to protect against some types of risk, but assumed away systemic conditions that wiped these hedges out like a well thrown bowling ball scoring a strike. Even for Fukushima

Daiichi where earthquake and tsunami risks were extensively considered, an event the magnitude of Tōhoku was not believed possible.

All evidence should be used for risk assessment – You may wonder why I allowed the "was risk assessed" question to be answered affirmatively for Fukushima Daiichi when I said earlier that a magnitude 9.0 quake was not thought possible by the plant designers. Remember that I also said that the design basis earthquake (DBE) was set using data from the century or so that accurate records have been kept. But there is also less rigorous evidence available from earlier times indicating that a great quake and tsunami occurred in the Fukushima region in 869 AD. Although this event was over a thousand years ago, that still gives it an observed frequency of about 1×10^{-3} per year which is a very high level for such a severe earthquake. If this evidence had been considered in the original plant design, things may have been done differently.

Complex, active safeguards aren't bulletproof – The Macondo team appears to have believed that the blowout preventer eliminated risk. I think this over placed faith in the BOP encouraged reckless well control decisions.

I will discuss ways to keep from making mistakes like these when performing risk assessments later in Part III. But I want to conclude the initial report card discussion by making the broad conclusion that the three catastrophes that we examined happened because their risk management systems lacked the necessary competence and professionalism needed to prevent and/or mitigate these events.

Chapter 5 - IN SEARCH OF PROFESSIONAL RISK MANAGEMENT

To reiterate the point I made at the conclusion of the last chapter, the risk management for each of our three report card events lacked the necessary competence and professionalism needed to prevent or mitigate these events. So how was this allowed to happen?

I believe that poor risk management practices found in our report card case studies happen first and foremost because risk management is more often regarded as a function performed by subject matter experts (SMEs) within a more established discipline or industry than it is regarded as an independent discipline practiced by specialists in risk management. This was clearly the case in all three of our report card events. To be sure, subject matter expertise is needed to do good risk management. But without the involvement of people with independent and objective risk management expertise, actual practices can vary widely with some industries doing good work while others address risk carelessly or even dishonestly just to provide a veneer of assurance for too likely to be victims.

In fact, I think my own career story lends support to this hypothesis.

My career in risk management began, as I think many have, without a lot of thought or planning. In truth, I was just standing in the right (or wrong) spot at the right (or wrong) time. It was March 1979 and I was a young engineer quite happily working as part of a large team trying to build and license the Midland Nuclear Power Plant, in Midland, Michigan. Although the total project team was quite large (5,000+), most were employees of the engineer/constructor, Bechtel Power Corporation or one of the major equipment suppliers. I was part of the relatively small (<50) team representing the eventual plant owner/operator, Consumers Power Company (now Consumers Energy) and my main responsibility was oversight of the design, licensing, and construction of the non-nuclear

39

mechanical systems. These include systems you would find in any steam power plant, regardless of the heat source. You nerds reading this would know them as the main turbine, main condenser, main feedwater, and main steam systems, among others. But Midland was to be a very special nuclear power plant, one that would produce not just electricity but also supply the neighboring Dow Chemical Company with 4 million pounds per hour of steam to operate their vast chemical production operations in Midland. Yes, I know, they could make toothpaste that glows in the dark!

To provide this "process steam" Midland was equipped with a special tertiary[1] steam system that could draw steam from either of the two nuclear reactors to supply Dow, even if the electric generators were not running. It was this part of the plant that occupied most of my attention up to this point. If you haven't already made the connection, March 25th, 1979, was the start of the infamous accident at Three Mile Island, unit 2 (TMI-2).

TMI and Midland were "sister plants" so called because they shared essentially identical Nuclear Steam Supply Systems made by the Babcock & Wilcox Corporation (B&W). This combined with the fact that Midland was still under construction and did not yet have a license from the U. S. Nuclear Regulatory Commission (NRC) to operate to made the political environment suddenly more anti-nuclear and very difficult for the Midland project. In response, the Consumers Power senior management decided to aggressively pursue the completion of Midland. One aspect of this strategy was to respond very quickly and comprehensively to any and all requests from the NRC for additional analyses or upgrades to the plant design[2]. This strategy impacted me very directly almost immediately.

---

[1] Tertiary because the Midland Nuclear Steam Supply Systems (NSSSs) were Pressurized Water Reactors (PWRs) that use Steam Generators to separate the primary and secondary steam systems inside the reactor building.
[2] Up to this point, it was customary to negotiate with the NRC to minimize changes.

Among the "non-nuclear" systems in my portfolio was "Auxiliary Feedwater" (AFW), which is a system used during plant start up and shut down, and during some accident conditions, to supply water to the steam generators inside the reactor building. Failure of the AFW system at TMI-2 to operate as required was one of the first major events in a series of equipment failures and operator errors that would eventually lead to core melt.

Soon after the accident, the NRC requested all plants to assess the reliability of their AFW systems. Midland jumped to respond. Being the owner's system engineer for AFW, I soon found myself in a whole new world. Up to this point, the reliability of a system was judged by the degree to which it complied with deterministic design criteria. These requirements were things like the number of redundant components, automatic starting, and more. In general, a system with more redundant components and more automatic controls was assumed to be more reliable. But now we (meaning me) were asked to make a quantitative assessment of system reliability so that, regardless of the design features, the system could be shown to be capable of performing above a goal set by the NRC.

This turned out to be a lot more than a technical task and because of the importance of this issue to overall project, I got a lot of help. I went from a simple engineer working in the guts of a big corporation to a new face sitting at the table across from the President and CEO of the company explaining what was being done to respond to this and other TMI related issues[3]. By far the most significant help I received were introductions to people who already knew something about reliability analysis and risk assessment that were able to come to my rescue and help complete the needed analysis. Included in this group were Dr. Norm Rasmussen from MIT plus Dr. B. John Garrick and Dr. Stan Kaplan from Pickard, Lowe, & Garrick (PLG), Inc. The quantitative risk assessment concepts

---

[3] Some offices really do have mahogany paneling!

and methods I learned from them made it possible to perform the AFW analysis as well as the Probabilistic Risk Analysis (PRA) of the entire Midland Plant that followed plus the many other applications I will talk about later in this book.

Alas, these efforts and those of the many others who worked on Midland were not sufficient. In July 1984, the project collapsed under the combined weight of unresolved licensing issues and cost overruns. All major elements of the plant were complete before cancellation and it still stands today as a colossal multi-billion dollar monument to failure.

From this experience I went on to actually work for PLG to help perform PRAs on other more successful nuclear plants and took it upon myself to study how quantitative risk analysis could help to prevent other failures of large, complex projects like Midland. This broader capability was especially useful during my later years at Los Alamos National Lab where I was able to work on very challenging risk management assignments, some of which I might even talk about later.

But the real purpose of telling this story is to point out how my path to the practice of risk management began with specific subject matter expertise, nuclear power, and then I learned how to perform risk analysis within that field and beyond. For too many others, however, I fear that they never practice beyond the narrow application area where they begin and never study risk management as an independent science.

Going beyond my own experience, I did some additional home work to look more broadly at the question of professionalism in risk management. What I found was that a vocation is expected to pass certain tests or exhibit specific characteristics before being called a profession. The following four characteristics represent a minimal but fair test for professional status.

1. Formal education requirements as evidenced by degree programs at accredited educational institutions

2. A professional association that includes a code of professional conduct or ethics and the licensing and certification of practitioners

3. Self recognition – individuals identify themselves first as members of the profession rather than employees of an organization

4. Public recognition – A sidewalk survey should find that a broad cross section of people can generally describe the skills and responsibilities of the profession.

So let's examine how risk management stacks up as a profession by looking at each characteristic.

Formal educational degree programs – The score on this criterion is a definite NO. I found perhaps a dozen institutions that offer any degree programs in risk management and all were in specific risk management applications. These include insurance risk, catastrophe risk, financial risk, business enterprise risk, business continuity risk, and healthcare risk. The problem is that these programs are primarily about the parent subject, not the discipline of risk management. I think one difficulty comes from the fact that risk assessment has no clear home at the college level in the typical academic hierarchy. As a result, each major college or school (engineering, business, medicine, etc) may offer some courses or programs that include risk analysis and risk management, but always only within the context of their core subject area.

A professional association – The score for this criterion is a NO, not really. Several noteworthy organizations address risk management professionalism within focused application areas. Among the largest are the Global Association of Risk Professionals (GARP), the Professional Risk Managers' International Association (PRMIA), and the Risk Management Association (RMA) that all focus on aspects of financial risk management. So much for the biggest being the best. Another very large organization with a risk management branch is the Project Management Institute (PMI) for project risk management. In addition, many other professional organizations include risk management as a special subject pertaining to their core discipline.

The only association that has any real ambition to reach across existing disciplines lines to provide a common forum for exchanging knowledge and advancing the state-of-the-art in risk management is the Society for Risk Analysis (SRA). Unfortunately, this organization has only about two thousand members and focuses primarily on risks to human health and the environment. But I think it is the best candidate to become the big tent for a wider spectrum of risk management professionals.

Recognition – Both self and public recognition are soft or qualitative criteria that are open to interpretation but still very important. They are also not completely independent (a subject we will discuss in more detail later). Even if an individual considers him or herself to be a professional, they might not use their professional status as a primary identifier if they doubt that it would be recognized. Having just retired from full time employment and moved to a new community, I personally have done this. First, describing myself as an engineer and then adding that I specialize in risk management. In a different setting, however, I might feel confident in introducing myself as a risk analyst. So, perhaps it is the state of public recognition for risk management that we should look at first. One place I thought to look for public recognition of risk management was employment ads. If risk analyst or risk manager is known well enough to be used to define a job category, then maybe I can say we have passed the recognition test for professional status.

To test this idea, I went to Monster.com, a large all-encompassing web site for job seekers and looked for risk analyst or risk manager. I got 2,900 hits for risk analyst or risk manager which I think indicates a good level of recognition at least for the titles. However, I could not tell what percentage of the total listings this represented. I also know that there are many more job posting sites that serve specific industries. For example, nuclear risk assessment openings can be found on the jobs page of the American Nuclear Society (ANS) web site. But overall, I think this data demonstrates that risk management is at least on its way to passing the public recognition test.

Also derived from the Monster job search was a breakdown of the hits by generic job categories defined by Monster. The exhibit below shows the results of this categorization. Note the great diversity of application areas for risk management.

Exhibit 5-1 Risk Management Job Adds by Industry

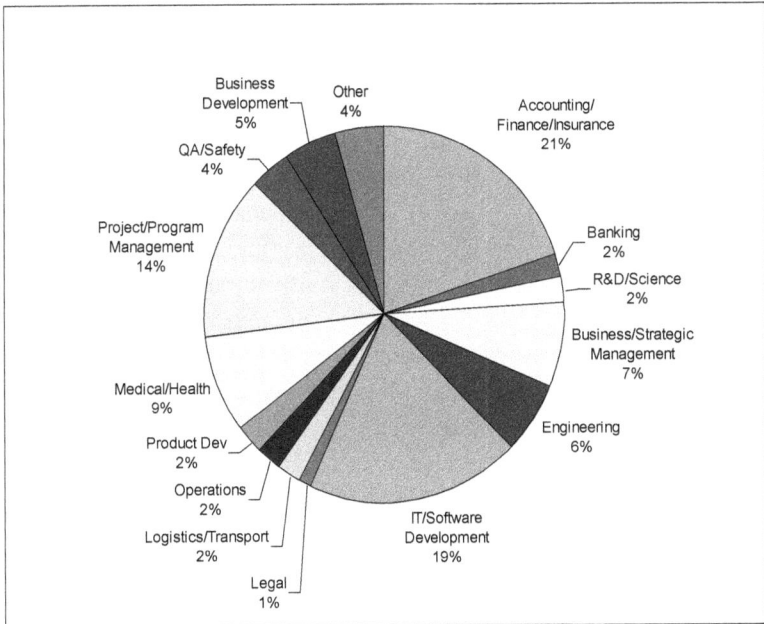

In summary then, here are the results of the profession test for risk management.

- Only a few universities offer any degree programs in risk management and then only as supplements to a core subject (example: business continuity risk at a business school).
- Several professional associations serve different application areas for risk management, but there is no strong unifying association that bridges all areas of risk management.

45

- There is significant public recognition for risk management but it probably has not reached par with more established professions.
- Based on a non-rigorous sample of employment adds, the risk management application areas in greatest demand are finance, IT/software development, and program/project management.

Based on this information, it's hard to make the case that the people assessing and managing risk in these very different application areas are united through common educational experiences or professional associations into a clearly recognizable profession.

But moving beyond the initial question of whether or not risk management can currently be called a professional discipline, the more important question becomes; should it be raised to a higher level of professional competence? I think our three report card case studies provide convincing evidence that the answer is YES! Of course risk management is a skill that all competent managers need to practice at some level. But when the consequences of risk management failure are catastrophic to society in general, a higher level of competence and professionalism needs to be applied. Each of our case studies revealed fundamental errors in risk management that could have been avoided.

So where do we go from here? We've seen that there are significant risks out there that threaten us both individually and collectively and that at least some of these risks have not been managed as well as they should have been. Plus, there is no reliable place the average person can go to get objective, professional quality information on risk issues they may care about to judge the quality of available risk information. Putting it more simply, it's a jungle out there and you are on our own! Be careful!

But I think I can help. In the next part of the book we are going to delve into the process of risk management and how it should be done. We'll do this not with the objective of making you an expert risk analyst but of giving you a competitive advantage in the jungle by being able to recognize signs that indicate how well risks you care about are being managed, or not. Remember the old risk management adage; you don't need to run faster than the bear, you only need to run faster than the other guy.

Part II – Understanding Risk Management

Chapter 6 - RISK MANAGEMENT 101

So, if the principle of *caveat emptor* rules in the risk management jungle, what does a person need to know to survive? The next two parts of this book will attempt to answer that question. First, we will lay out some basic concepts and principles that will help you to understand the risk management process and introduce a language that allows us to communicate risk in a consistent way. Next, we will review a spectrum of methods and tools that can be used for performing risk analysis. Then we will delve into what risk assessment results look like and how to use them appropriately. Finally, in Part III we will look at some of the common problems that can cause risk assessment results to be wrong and how to spot these problems before it's too late. Although it is necessary to get somewhat technical in discussing these topics, the focus throughout will be on making the reader a better consumer of risk management information. If you are inspired to become an expert risk analyst, I'll point to references along the way that will give you a start in that direction.

So let's begin. If there should be only one thing you understand clearly and remember forever from this book, let it be this: good risk management is not indicated by a magic analysis tool or complex mathematics, you will recognize it first and foremost as a disciplined process that governs the behavior of a person or organization.

The Exhibit 6-1 shows a simple generic flowchart of the risk management process. Before we discuss the piece parts of this flowchart, please take a minute or two and walk through it yourself. Now look at the flowchart again and mentally replace the word *risk* with another that holds a special interest for you. Try using *safety, quality, security, cost,* or just *performance*. As you can see, this flowchart represents the generic process for managing anything we really care about. The message this flowchart delivers is simple but profound; risk is managed as an integral part of any deliberate action. Risk management is not a separate activity isolated from general management. Risk management is simply one element of trying to foresee and control future events. In particular, events that could produce unwanted outcomes contrary to the intentions of our planned actions.

Oops, you're thinking that this statement conflicts with my conclusion from Part I that says risk management should be done by professional risk analysts. No, the lesson from Part I is that when the risk analysis done by subject matter experts indicates that scenarios from the planned action could result in societal level consequences, a higher *professional* level of risk management is called for in addition to the normal in-house process. Going beyond just extreme consequences, however, I do believe that the overall management process would benefit from professional level risk management expertise.

Exhibit 6-1 Risk Management Process Flowchart

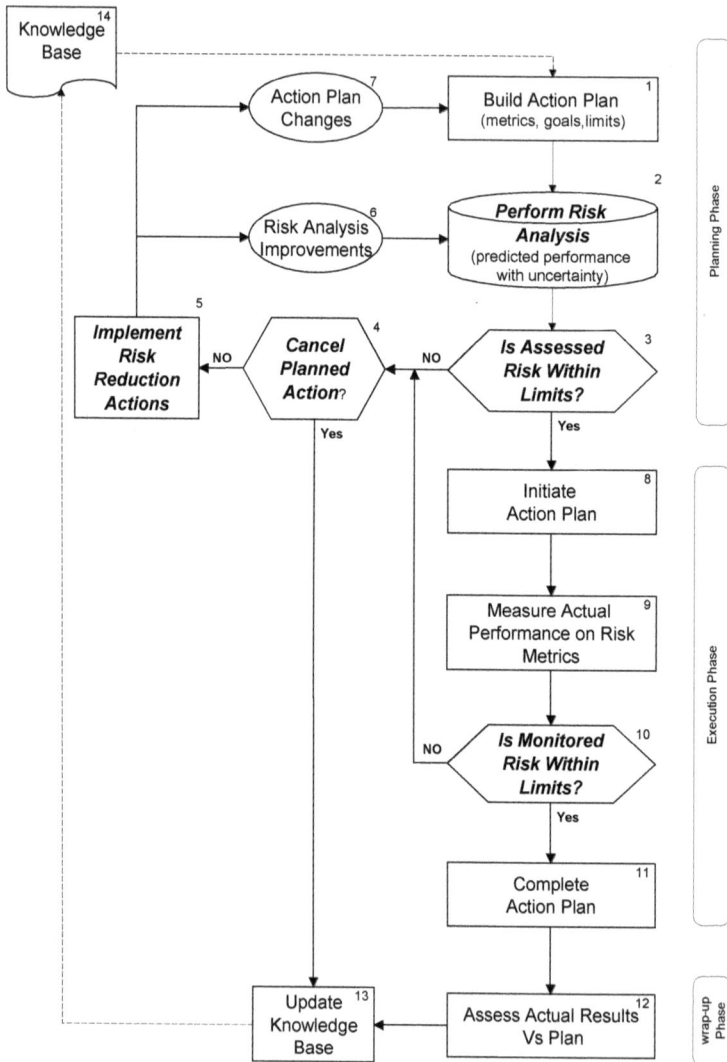

So let's take a closer look at some of the components of the risk management process. Like any management activity, risk management begins with a plan (1) for proposed action. More specifically, what a risk analysis needs from the primary action plan is clear definition of *success* for the planned activity. Risk, like any other management process, needs to focus on performance that can be measured. The proposed action plan needs to specify these metrics (1) and the performance levels that define success and failure for the proposed actions. Sometimes failure can be defined using the same metrics as success. An obvious example would be a loss, rather than a gain in the price of an investment. In other cases, metrics may be needed that specifically focus on risk. Good examples of such metrics from our report card cases would have been blowout likelihood for Macondo and core melt frequency for the Fukushima reactors. But I found no evidence that either of these metrics were used to assess risk for those events.

Armed with a definitive plan for success and the needed metrics to define both success and possible failure, the analysis (2) of possible unwanted outcomes can now be performed. Again, this is done in conjunction with the assessment of cost, schedule, marketing, sales, and all other performance metrics. As indicated in the flowchart the output of the risk analysis (2) includes not only estimated values for performance on relevant metrics but also some assessment of the uncertainty in the predicted point values. For an example of what I am talking about here, please look back at Exhibit 3-3. Here we can see that although specific numbers or *point values* were calculated for both the load (L) and capacity (C) in this example, the full story of the risk was only revealed when we also considered the uncertainty in L and C. In Chapter 7 and Part III we will look at how to actually do risk analyses, including uncertainty, in more depth.

Using the predicted performance values and uncertainty from the risk analysis we can then ask if the assessed risk is acceptably low before proceeding with any planned actions (3). To do this, we need to set goals and/or limits for acceptable performance on the selected metrics. If the predicted risk is not deemed acceptable, then the planned action can be cancelled (4), or improvements made to the risk analysis (6), the action plan (7), or both to bring the risk down to acceptable levels. Often multiple iterations through the risk reduction loop are needed before the planned actions are initiated. While the action plan should provide a clear definition of what performance is needed for success, the question of how to set these go/no-go hurdles for performance on risk metrics and how to answer the cancellation questions in the flowchart require a somewhat different perspective that we will address more fully in Chapter 8.

Once underway (8), the actual performance (9) for all metrics needs to be monitored against what was predicted (10) to be sure no unexpected deviation or variance from predicted values occurs. If it does, then a return to the risk reduction loop used during planning is needed. Risk reduction actions needed during the execution phase can be very painful. In the planning phase of any activity, changes come relatively easily because they can be made "on paper". Once underway however, changes may be needed to things already "in concrete". In the Macondo case study we saw many changes made to the drilling plan during the execution phase but with no consideration of the possible impacts on blowout risk.

Upon completion of the execution phase of the activity (11), it is time to look back and compare the actual performance experienced on the risk metrics with predictions made during planning plus any additions made during execution (12). The purpose behind this step in the risk management process is not merely to assess rewards or penalties for the just completed activity, but to allow the new performance data and lessons learned to be added (13) to the body of knowledge (14) that forms the foundation for planning the next set of activities of the kind just completed. Over time, this steady updating of the knowledge base enables better performance on risk and all other metrics.

So what have we accomplished by laying out and discussing risk management as a process before getting into any of the nitty-gritty of risk assessment? Well, we have set the stage for that discussion by establishing the role risk assessment plays in the overall risk management process. But more importantly, you already have taken a first step in understanding what to look for when someone claims to be managing risk. For example, without having any special knowledge of well drilling or risk assessment methods, you could have examined the plans for Macondo and asked to see the metrics being used to measure blowout risk. With the only possible responses to the question being some variant of "don't worry" or "the dog ate my homework", you would already have a good basis to be skeptical about the risk of a blowout. In contrast, if the drilling team was able to respond to your question with actual evidence indicating that they were using a risk management process, you could begin to feel better. But we are not going to stop here. Next, we will add to your toolkit by taking a step into the realm of risk assessment.

Chapter 7 - PERFORMING RISK ASSESSMENTS

Basic Concepts and Definitions

Once it can be established that at least a semblance of process exists to manage risk, we can now turn our attention to the role and importance of risk assessment within the general process of managing risk. By referring back to Exhibit 6-1 we can see that the risk assessment needs information inputs from the general action plan and outputs predictions of performance on selected metrics, including uncertainty. While the Action Plan provides a measurable definition of success for the planned activity, it is the job of the risk analysis to consider and evaluate possible unwanted outcomes. Boiled down to the essentials, a risk assessment answers three fundamental questions.

1. What can go wrong with the as-planned scenario?
2. How likely is this to occur?
3. What consequences are suffered if it does happen?

Organizing risk assessment around this seemingly simple triplet of questions was first done in the seminal paper *On The Quantitative Definition of Risk* authored by two key mentors of my risk management career, Stan Kaplan and B. John Garrick. This paper is considered by many to be the Rosetta Stone document that establishes the basic concepts and principles of modern quantitative risk management. It was published as the first paper in the first issue of *Risk Analysis*, the journal of the Society of Risk Analysis in 1981. I will borrow extensively from this paper to get us started but those craving a more rigorous mathematical treatment of risk assessment should get your own copy and read it completely.

Returning to the triplet of questions, a risk assessment can then be defined as a list of answers to these questions. The answers to question number one are risk *scenarios* that describe a series of events leading from a starting point or *initiating event* to a stable final condition called an *end state*. A simple example scenario is the coin toss where the initiating event is the toss of the coin and the possible end states for the scenario are heads and tails. The scenario list includes all possible results for the planned activities spanning end states for both success and failure.

The answers to question number two, likelihood, can come in several formats. In *quantitative risk assessments*, likelihood can be expressed as a *frequency*, that is the number of events observed in a measured number of trials (N/T) or as the number of events observed per unit of time (e.g. deaths per year). There are also situations where it is useful to set the initiating event frequency equal to 1.0 and then have the end state results be *conditional probabilities* with values between zero and 1.0.

Risk assessment methods have also been developed that require only a qualitative expression of likelihood. In these methods that we will look at in more depth later, likelihood is ranked against a benchmark event (more than, about the same, less than) or a generic scale (high, medium, low). As a result, these types of analyses are called *qualitative risk assessments*.

The third question, consequences, must be answered using one or more *consequence metrics* that measure the injury or loss incurred from a risk scenario. Examples from our report card case studies include human deaths, gallons of oil spilled, and monetary loss. As with likelihood, consequences can be expressed quantitatively using defined metrics or qualitatively using relative ranking scales. We will take a closer look at how risk analysis results are displayed and used in Chapter 8.

To complete the risk assessment process, we need to address the additional question of how uncertainty affects the answers to the first three questions. To do this, we will express our level of confidence in the answers to each of the triplet questions as a *probability*. The scale we use to express probability ranges from zero to 1.0 and it is fully expressed with a curve that describes the probability density across this range for the parameter of interest. I'll say more about the concept of probability in Chapter 8.

The Exhibit 7-1 summarizes our first level description of the risk assessment process. Next we will look a little deeper into each of the four tasks in the process to provide an overview of how they are actually done. Also, definitions for many of the words shown in italics in this book are repeated in the glossary located in an appendix at the end of this book for future easy reference.

Exhibit 7-1 - Risk Analysis 101

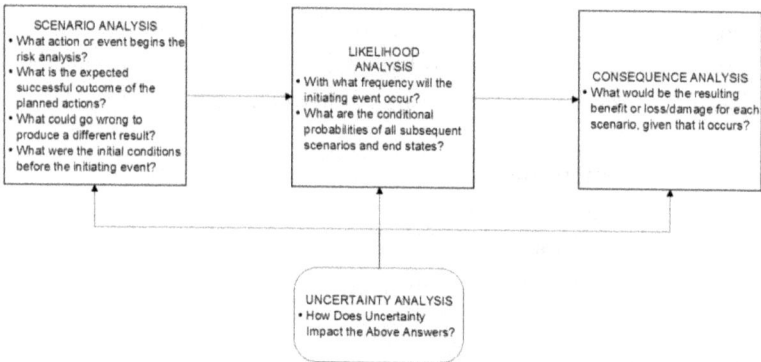

```
┌──────────────────────────┐      ┌──────────────────────────┐      ┌──────────────────────────┐
│    SCENARIO ANALYSIS     │      │                          │      │                          │
│ • What action or event   │      │       LIKELIHOOD         │      │                          │
│   begins the risk        │      │        ANALYSIS          │      │  CONSEQUENCE ANALYSIS    │
│   analysis?              │      │ • With what frequency    │      │ • What would be the      │
│ • What is the expected   │      │   will the initiating    │      │   resulting benefit or   │
│   successful outcome of  │      │   event occur?           │      │   loss/damage for each   │
│   the planned actions?   │      │ • What are the           │      │   scenario, given that   │
│ • What could go wrong to │      │   conditional            │      │   it occurs?             │
│   produce a different    │      │   probabilities of all   │      │                          │
│   result?                │      │   subsequent scenarios   │      │                          │
│ • What were the initial  │      │   and end states?        │      │                          │
│   conditions before the  │      │                          │      │                          │
│   initiating event?      │      │                          │      │                          │
└──────────────────────────┘      └──────────────────────────┘      └──────────────────────────┘

                          ┌──────────────────────────┐
                          │   UNCERTAINTY ANALYSIS   │
                          │ • How Does Uncertainty   │
                          │   Impact the Above       │
                          │   Answers?               │
                          └──────────────────────────┘
```

Scenario Analysis – Provides a description of the action or event that begins the risk analysis and the possible scenarios that could evolve following the initiating event. This includes a description of the "as planned" scenario which defines success for the endeavor under study as well as failure scenarios which end in various degrees of injury, loss, or damage.

Scenario analysis also includes a definition of the problem under study and a listing of the assumptions and boundary conditions that define the external environment under which the proposed activities will be evaluated.

Likelihood Analysis – Determines the resulting frequency of each possible scenario from the Scenario Analysis. The sum of all the scenario frequencies must equal the initiating event frequency.

Consequence Analysis – Assesses the resulting damage or loss that would be realized for each scenario, given that it occurs. The results of the risk analysis are then obtained by summing all the conditional damages by the frequencies of the corresponding scenarios.

Uncertainty Analysis – The confidence with which the likelihood analysis and consequence analysis questions can be answered, this is expressed in terms of probability.

Answering three questions seems pretty straightforward but if you sit down and try to compile a scenario list for anything beyond the most trivial of activities, you will quickly realize that this is difficult and could take a while. As a result, there are many methods and tools that have been developed to organize and assist the process. In the balance of this chapter I will give an overview of a spectrum of methods, but only with the objective of introducing you to the various approaches and making you a better consumer of risk analyses, not to make you a proficient analyst. Although there are really only a few main categories of risk assessment methods, you may encounter many variants of these general methods using many different names. Some of these variations come merely from adapting a method to a new application area but sometimes new names are used just in an attempt to gain a degree of uniqueness (old wine in a new bottle).

To begin our review of risk assessment methods let's begin with some steps essential to all methods.

Define the System
First, remember from our risk management process flowchart that what we are doing here is trying to predict the outcome of future actions using imperfect knowledge. The focus of the analysis will be some defined *system* meaning an entity comprised of interacting discrete elements functioning to achieve some beneficial objective. The elements making up the system can be hardware, software, natural, or human and will require a variety of analysis tools that will need to work in concert, just like the system elements themselves, to present a credible forecast of the future. A critical first step is to define

the system under study, to enumerate its elements and to identify its boundaries through which it interacts with the external (to the system) environment. A nuclear power plant is an example of a system that is composed of scores of plant systems like reactor protection and main feed water that are in turn composed of millions of subsystems, components, and parts. Other more common systems are all around us. The internet is a massive communication system. Our homes are served daily by electric power, water, sewer, and natural gas systems. Our manufacturing systems produce all manner of goods. The U.S. and global financial systems have been the focus of much attention in recent times for their not-so-good operation. On a smaller scale, your car is a system, as is the dishwasher, and every commercial kitchen.

Define Success

As stated earlier, risk, like any other management process, needs to focus on performance that can be measured. Success for the as planned operation of the subject system needs to be defined using measurable performance metrics. Failure also needs to be specified in a measurable way. Sometimes failure can be defined using the same metrics as success. An obvious example would be a loss, rather than a gain in the price of an investment. In other cases, metrics may be needed that specifically focus on risk. Candidate risk metrics from our report card cases would have been blowout likelihood for Macondo and core melt frequency for the Fukushima reactors. But schedule and cost were also obviously important metrics for the Macondo team. So even if a risk assessment is focused on a single performance metric, the success or failure of an overall enterprise always involves multiple performance metrics and decisions may need input from multiple risk assessments.

Also important to the definition of success metrics is the role of time in the proposed analysis. Since the issue of time can only be addressed comprehensively with quantitative risk analysis methods, we will delay further discussion of this topic for a few pages.

Understand the Physics

Before we can go any farther in constructing a risk assessment, a fundamental understanding of the physics of the system under study is needed. By "physics" I mean the basic science of how it is constructed and how it operates, under both normal and abnormal conditions. This knowledge generally comes to the risk analysis through people who I have already labeled "subject matter experts" or SMEs, but it's also important to know the source of their knowledge. System knowledge can come from several sources. Existing systems should have actual performance data and SMEs with hands-on system operating experience. But if the system has not been built yet or the risk analysis extends beyond existing data and normal operations into operating regimes where there is no experience, other information sources are needed. To understand system behavior under extreme stress, the risk analysis team may need to perform controlled tests on the system or scale models of the system. In addition, modern computational tools often allow mathematical models to be built that can simulate physical system operation and behavior under stress. These tools are often used in combination with scenario modeling tools that we will be discussing shortly to build the complete story of system risk.

Overview of Risk Assessment Methods

Now that the risk management problem has been adequately defined, we can move forward to assemble the scenario list. I have already mentioned that risk assessment methods can be categorized by whether they assess likelihood qualitatively or quantitatively. Another way to categorize risk assessment methods is by their logical approach to the search for scenarios. Inductive analysis methods walk through a system in some manner searching for things that can go wrong. Deductive analysis methods postulate an unwanted event or condition and search for how it could be made to happen. The triplet approach discussed above is conceptually inductive and a rich variety of risk assessment tools have been fashioned using this approach whereas the primary deductive risk assessment tools are the *fault tree* and its less formal cousin, the *master logic diagram*.

In practice, comprehensive risk assessments utilize both inductive and deductive methods to fully examine a complex system. The exhibit on the next page lists a spectrum of risk assessment methods categorized by logical approach and results format.

Exhibit 7-2 Risk Assessment Methods

		Logic Concept	
		Inductive	**Deductive**
Desired Results	**Qualitative**	What If Analysis Failure Mode & Effects Analysis Hazards and Operability Study Preliminary Hazards Analysis	Master Logic Diagram
	Quantitative	Event Tree Monte Carlo Simulation System Simulation	Fault Tree

I will begin by dividing risk assessment methods into two categories already mentioned: qualitative and quantitative.

Qualitative Risk Assessment Methods

Qualitative risk assessment methods seek to rank risk on a relative scale against a benchmark event (more than, about the same, less than) or a generic scale (high, medium, low). The items to be ranked can be scenarios, events, conditions, projects, issues, or any coherent list of items. Qualitative risk assessment methods can be further divided into those that rank risk directly and those that rank likelihood and consequence separately and then use a *risk matrix* to determine the final risk categorization. Another variant on risk ranking scales uses a single long scale (5+ categories) and then may group several of these categories together to bin down to a more generic final high, medium, low type ranking (see Exhibit 7-7). Similar qualitative ranking methods are also used in decision analysis to assess other aspects of performance besides risk. This boundary between risk assessment and decision analysis is fuzzy for good reason – they are one and the same and I will talk more about this point later..

Examples of these ranking systems are shown in the following exhibits.

Exhibit 7-3 Example Direct Risk Assignment Scale

PERFORMANCE MEASURE		RANKING SCALE		
DESCRIPTION	DISCUSSION	HIGH (1)	MEDIUM (3)	LOW (5)
Implementation Risk	This factor measures the risk that planned actions will not be completed as scheduled and/or will cost more than estimated. Potential consequences include extended operations without problem resolution and failure to complete planned actions. It is measured qualitatively, in absolute terms.	Proposed actions are complex and/or not well defined, risks of delays and/or a cost overrun are high.	Proposed actions are somewhat complex but are well defined, risks of delays and/or a cost overrun are medium.	Proposed actions are straightforward and well defined, risks of delays and/or a cost overrun are low.

Exhibit 7-4 Example Likelihood Assignment Scale

I (1 to 0.1)	Normal Operations: frequency as often as once in 10 operating years or at least once in 10 similar facilities operated for 1 year.
II (0.1 to .01)	Anticipated Events: frequency between 1 in 100 years and 1 in 10 operating years or at least once in 100 similar facilities operated for 1 year.
III (10-2 to 10-4)	Unlikely: frequency between 1 in 100 years and 1 in 10,000 operating years or at least once in 10,000 similar facilities operated for 1 year.
IV (10-4 to 10-6)	Very Unlikely: frequency between 1 in 10,000 years and once in 1 million years or at least once in a million similar facilities operated for 1 year.
V	Improbable: frequency of less than once in a million years.

Exhibit 7-5 Example Consequence Assignment Scale

	Maximum Possible Consequences		
Category	Public Health	Worker Health	Environment
A	No significant offsite impact.	Minor or no injury and no disability.	Minor or no contamination of originating facility/ activity; no onsite contamination. No offsite contamination.
B	Irritation or discomfort but no permanent health effects.	Lost-time injury but no disability. Radiation uptake or dose causing temporary radiation worker restriction.	Significant contamination of originating facility/activity, minor onsite contamination. No offsite contamination.
C	Long-term health effects.	Severe injury or disability. Radiation > MPBB uptake.	Moderate-to-significant onsite-only contamination and/or minor offsite contamination.
D	Immediate health effects.	Loss of life.	Significant offsite contamination.

Exhibit 7-6 Example Risk Ranking Matrix

Risk Ranking Matrix				
Severity of Consequence	Likelihood of Consequence			
	A	B	C	D
I				
II				
III				
IV				
V				

Risk Rank	Recommendation
High	Unacceptable: Should be mitigated to Medium or Low as soon as possible.
Medium	Acceptable with Controls: Verify that procedures, controls, and safeguards are in place.
Low	Acceptable As Is: No action necessary.

Exhibit 7-7 Example Long Risk Ranking Scale

TECHNOLOGY RISK RANKING SCALE			
		Risk Rank	Description of Activities
H I G H	1	Basic Principles	This is the first level of technology readiness and includes fundamental scientific research. At this level, basic scientific principles are being studied analytically and/or experimentally. Examples might include paper studies of a technology's basic properties.
	2	Concept Formulated	Practical applications are beginning to be invented or identified. Applications are still speculative and there is no proof or detailed analysis to support assumptions. Examples might include applied research in a field of potential interest.
	3	Concept Demonstrated	Active research and development is initiated. This includes analytical and laboratory-based studies to physically validate analytical predictions of key elements of the technology. These studies and experiments should constitute "proof-of-concept" validation of the applications/concepts formulated at TRL 2. Examples include the study of separate elements of the technology that are not yet integrated or representative.
	4	Key Elements Demonstrated in Lab Environment	The key elements must be integrated to establish that the pieces will work together. The validation should be consistent with the requirements of potential applications, but it is relatively low-fidelity when compared to a final product.
M E D	5	Key Elements Demonstrated in Relevant Environment	Fidelity of the key elements increases significantly. Key elements are integrated with realistic supporting elements so that the technology can be tested and demonstrated in simulated or actual environments.
	6	Representative Deliverable Demonstrated in Relevant or Operational Environment	Represents a major step in a technology's demonstrated readiness. Examples include testing a prototype or representative of a deliverable in a high-fidelity, simulated environment or actual environment.
L O W	7	Final Development Deliverable Demonstrated in Operational Environment	Development version of the deliverable is near or at the planned operational system. This represents a significant step beyond TRL 6 and requires the demonstration of an actual development version of the deliverable in the operational environment. Manufacturing line.
	8	Deliverable Qualified Through Test & Demonstration	The technology has been proven to work in its final form under expected conditions. In almost all cases, this TRL represents the end of true system development. Examples include developmental test and evaluation of the actual deliverable in its intended application to validate that it meets design specifications.
	9	Operational Use of Deliverable	Application of the technology in its final form and under mission conditions such as those encountered in operational test and evaluation. In almost all cases, this is the end of the last bug fixing aspects of true system development. Examples include using the deliverable under operational mission conditions. This TRL does not include ongoing or planned product improvement of reusable systems.

Once the qualitative risk ranking system is selected, the items to be ranked need to be identified and the basis for assigning risk established. As indicated earlier, the items to be ranked can be scenarios, events, conditions, projects, issues, or any coherent list of items. And many times qualitative risk ranking is done for lists of items that are – just lists of items that someone wants prioritized. There is no problem at all with a list that is just a list, as long as this is recognized by all involved in the process. In other circumstances, the list needs to claim a degree of completeness. Looking back at the risk management process flowchart, we can see that if the risk assessment doesn't identify a potential problem, it will not get fixed. So when completeness is important several methods are available to aid the assessment process.

Failure Mode and Effects (FMEA) analysis is a method often used to examine a component or system for single point failures. In this analysis method, each part or component is examined for its possible failure modes and the likelihood and effects of the potential failure are documented. The likelihood of failure is based on historical data applicable to the problem and the effects are assessed by a competent subject matter expert using a problem specific consequence ranking scale similar to our examples above. FMEA and variants of this method are commonly used by the U.S. Department of Defense and NASA.

Some draw backs of the FMEA are the need for relevant component level failure data and its inability to identify multiple failure event scenarios. A very simple example of an FMEA analysis form is shown in the following Exhibit.

Exhibit 7-8 Example FMEA Document Form

Description	Function	Failure Mode	Cause of Failure	Effect of Failure	Corrective Action Detection	Crit./ Rank

source: NASA Lewis Research Center

Another qualitative risk ranking methodology widely used to evaluate risks in process based activities is the process hazards analysis (PHA). Two types of PHAs widely used are the Preliminary Hazards Analysis (also PHA) and the Hazards and Operability Study (HAZOP). These methodologies were widely used first in the chemical and petrochemical industries and were formalized in the 1970s by the Center for Chemical Process Safety (CCPS) which is a part of the American Institute of Chemical Engineers (AIChE)[4]. Process hazards analyses are organized around a systematic walk-through of a process flow diagram by a team composed of risk analysts and process specific experts. Together the team examines each step of the process for possible susceptibility to an extensive list of possible hazards searching to identify all scenarios that could result from potential accidents emanating from the activities involved in that step of the process. The potential consequences and a subjective estimate of the likelihood of each accident scenario are made from ranking tables like those in the previous exhibits. The assignment of the scenario to a risk category is made by using a predetermined risk matrix like that shown in Exhibit 7-5. A task flowchart for performing a PHA and an example of scenario level results from a PHA are shown in the following two exhibits.

---

[4] *Guidelines for Hazard Evaluation Procedures*, 3rd Edition, Center for Chemical Process Safety (CCPS), ISBN: 978-0-471-97815-2, April 2008

Exhibit 7-9 Preliminary Hazards Analysis Task Flowchart

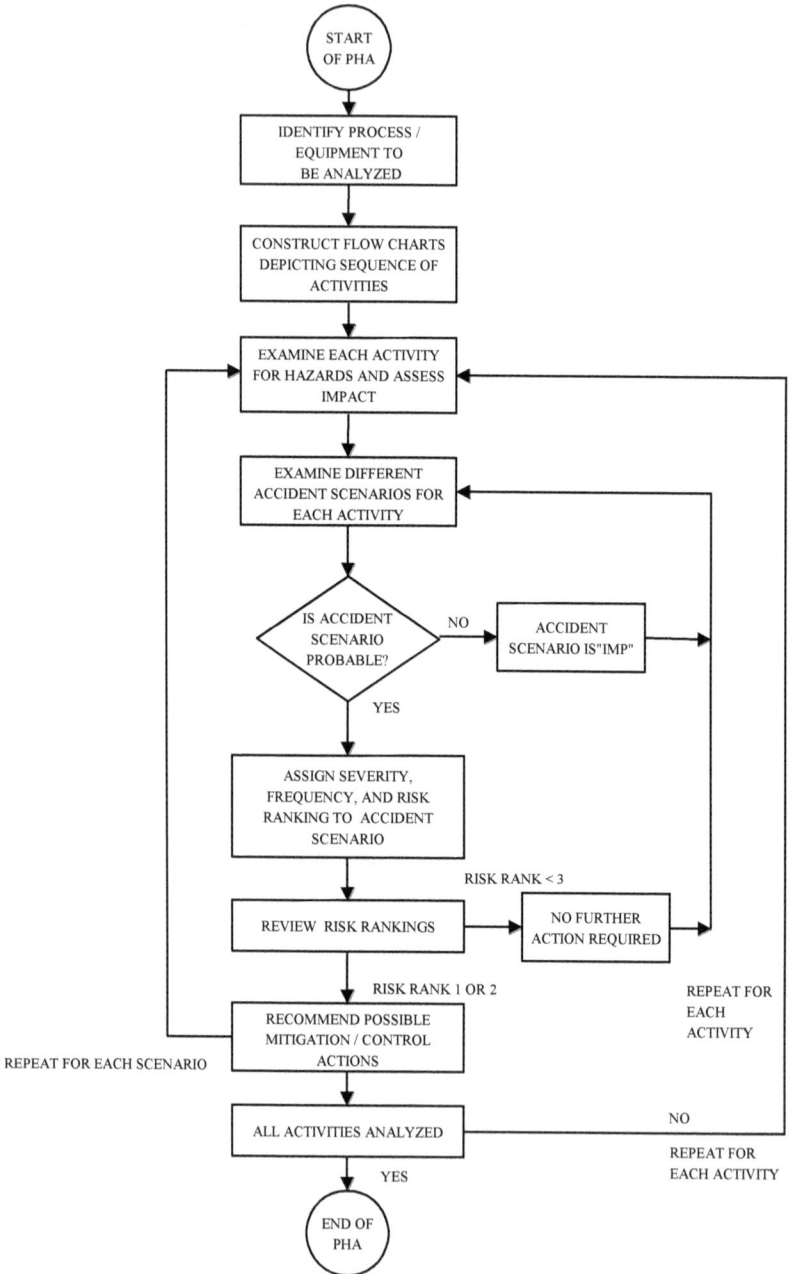

Exhibit 7-10 Example PHA Scenario Results

Node	Description of Scenario	Risk Rank	Freq Rank	Conseq Rank	Recommendations	Revised Risk Rank	Revised Freq Rank	Revised Conseq Rank
CY12	CYANIDE PLATING WASTE PUMPED TO WRONG LOCATION AND MIXED WITH NONCOMPATIBLE MATERIAL (I.E., WASTE DRUM, WASTE WATER SYSTEM, CHEMICAL MIX AND FEED TANK, CHEMICAL FEED DRUM OR THE DRY CHEMICAL FEEDER.) PLATING	1	II	A	(1) INSTALL CHECK VALVES ON OUTLET LINES OF THE CHEMICAL MIX FEED TANK, CHEMICAL FEED DRUM AND CHEMICAL PLATING WASTE DRUM (2) FOLLOW VALVE ALIGNMENT CHECKLIST PROCEDURE (3) VALVES SHOULD HAVE POSITION INDICATORS (4) OPERATORS EQUIPPED WITH PROTECTIVE CLOTHING AND RESPIRATOR (5) HAVE TWO OPERATORS CHECK VALVE POSITIONING (6) INSTALL INTERLOCK WHICH ALLOWS OPENING OF ONE VALVE AT A TIME	3	III	B (w)
HW7A	BREACH OF LEGACY CYLINDER OF DOUBTFUL INTEGRITY DURING STORAGE.	1	II	A	(1) DO NOT STORE LEGACY CYLINDERS IN HWTF AREA, (2) PROCESS LEGACY CYLINDERS WITHOUT INTERMEDIATE STORAGE, (3) PROVIDE SECONDARY CONTAINMENT FOR THE CYLINDERS, (4) CONSIDER ENCLOSING THE HWTF STORAGE AND PROVIDING HVAC AND SCRUBBER.	N/A	N/A	N/A
HWG	LOW INTENSITY SEISMIC EVENT WITH HORIZONTAL ACCELERATION OF 0.1 G.	1	II	A	(1) DEVELOP AND ENFORCE STRICT POLICY NOT TO STORE EXPLOSIVES OR SHOCK SENSITIVE MATERIALS IN THE BUILDING, (2) CONSIDER STORAGE OF SHOCK SENSITIVE IN A SEPARATE BUILDING IN A REMOTE LOCATION.	N/A	N/A	N/A
MW7A	MAJOR BREACH OF LEGACY CYLINDER OF DOUBTFUL INTEGRITY DURING STORAGE.	1	II	A	(1) DO NOT STORE LEGACY CYLINDERS IN THE MWSRF, (2) PROCESS LEGACY CYLINDERS WITHOUT INTERMEDIATE STORAGE, (3) PROVIDE SECONDARY CONTAINMENT WHEN TRANSPORTING LEGACY CYLINDERS.	N/A	N/A	N/A

Scenario level PHA results can be aggregated by risk rank, likelihood rank, or consequence rank to provide summary level results of the analysis. Any remaining "high" risk items can be placed on a *risk watch list* or register and tracked until reduced to a lower risk level.

The strengths of hazards analysis methods are relative simplicity in process and structure, its ability to address scenarios including human errors rather than just part or component failures, and the obvious relevance of results. Critical factors for success are good documentation for the process under study that include normal and emergency operating procedures, the participation of knowledgeable process experts, and a well-established operating experience base that can be used to benchmark the likelihood and consequence tables. Weaknesses come from not having the critical success factors in place and the normal vulnerability of bias in the subjective judgments of the process experts.

In the thirty plus years since hazards analysis type methods came into wide use they have been adapted to wide variety of applications ranging far away from their roots in the chemical and petrochemical industries. Unfortunately too many of the adopted applications have not paid attention to the critical success factors I list and have encountered problems in producing worthwhile results. Two notable risk matrix type applications that have not done well are project management and enterprise risk management.

Quantitative Risk Assessment Methods

The qualitative risk assessment methods we have looked at so far are capable only of ranking items or issues relative to each other or a generic scale. While such results can be useful, they are limited. In many cases a risk result of LOW or less than another item is just not adequate to answer the questions in the risk management process flowchart. For this we need an absolute measurement of risk that we can use to base cost/benefit and go/no-go judgments on. This brings us into the realm of quantitative risk assessment. Now we are going to consider methods that will aid in actually putting numbers to the scenario list we described earlier.

All that we said earlier about defining the system, selecting metrics for measuring success and failure, and understanding system physics still holds true. However, quantitative risk analysis also requires careful consideration of the importance of time in the analysis. Quantitative system analyses can be subdivided into two general categories, continuous or production type systems and once-through or mission type systems. Continuous or production systems are any activities that operate in a steady state controlled manner to perform a beneficial function. Examples that have been the focus of risk assessments include nuclear power plants, many manufacturing facilities, electric, oil and gas production and distribution systems, and the like. Once-through or mission systems are by contrast those with well-defined start and end points. Examples of these are a space shuttle mission, an airplane flight, and a project. The distinction between these two types of systems is important because it will influence the approach taken for structuring the scenario analysis, the search for initiating events, and the analysis quantification process.

For continuous systems it is typical to start the analysis with the system to be evaluated in normal steady state operation and then focus the risk assessment on events or conditions that could disturb the normal operations and cause the system to respond with an action or series of actions that could result in some degree of lost production and potential damage to the system itself, requiring repair. Risk for continuous systems will then be quantified over a unit of time (month, year, etc.). Initiating events will be those things that could happen to disturb the normal system operation and we will need to estimate the frequency with which they are expected to occur during the time period under study. If all the scenarios and their accompanying likelihood and consequences are then listed in order of increasing severity and plotted, a *risk curve* displaying the predicted maximum level of damage or loss that could occur at specific frequencies can be plotted that is the comprehensive result of the risk assessment for a specific consequence metric. Another common form of results comes from the convolution of the scenario frequencies and consequences. This is the *expected value* of the loss or damage resulting from the planned activity and is effectively the area under the risk curve. The expected value of the risk is expressed in units of loss or damage per unit time for the analysis ($/year or deaths/year).

By calculating the expected value of the loss or damage before and after the implementation of risk reduction actions, we can assess the loss or damage avoided by adoption of the risk reduction actions and compare this with the expected cost to judge their value.

The following Exhibit shows the basic form of a risk curve.

Exhibit 7-11 Example Risk Curve in Frequency Format

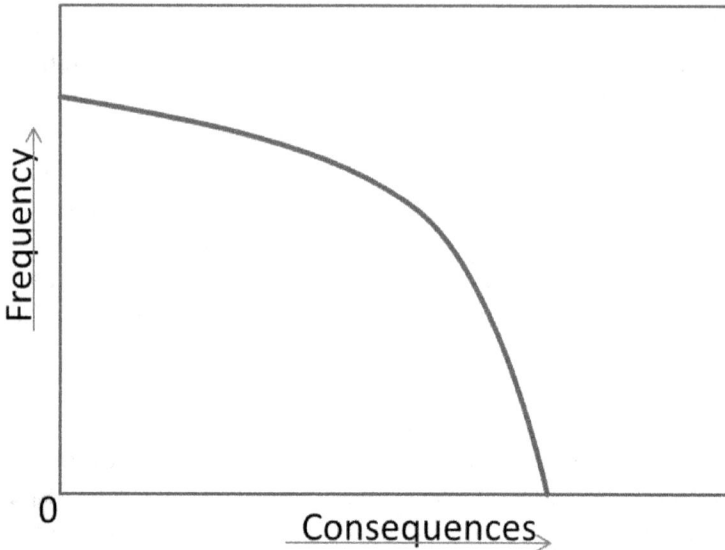

For mission type systems, the risk analysis usually initiates at the start of the mission and each subsequent activity along the path to completion is examined using the triplet of questions to identify possible outcomes other than success for the planned mission. For mission type analyses, risk will be calculated for the duration of the mission rather than a fixed unit of time. The duration of each activity and the overall mission is usually important not only for this reason but because duration is often an important performance metric by itself. All projects manage schedule duration as a primary performance metric. Other regularly repeated missions are still time critical. Payrolls must be ready on pay day and donuts are only going to fetch full price at breakfast. Thus, time is not just a unit used to quantify risk but is itself a risk metric. If the mission initiating event frequency is set at 1.0 and time duration calculated as a performance/risk metric then the result will be a plot of the probability of possible time durations. The Exhibit 7-12 illustrates such a result. This chart shows the cumulative probability of possible completion dates for a project. Thus, the later dates exhibit higher probabilities until virtual certainty of completion is reached at about 12/26. Other performance/risk metrics can be calculated and displayed in a similar manner.

Exhibit 7-12 Example Probability of Duration Risk Curve

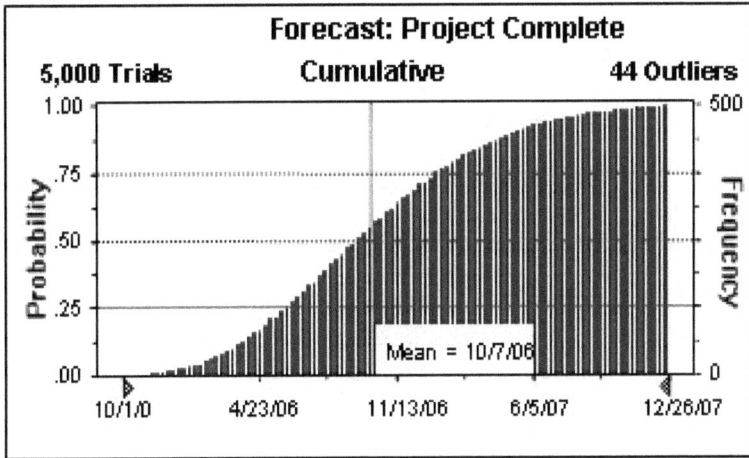

Also note that if system start-up and shut-down are potential sources of risk for continuous systems, they can be treated as mission analyses tacked onto the continuous system analysis.

I will discuss the forms and uses of results more in Chapter 9, but now let's take a closer look at the tools used to produce quantitative risk results.

Event Trees
Event tree modeling is the most direct and understandable method for quantitative risk analysis. An event tree is simply a diagram that logically resolves all possible outcomes from a causally ordered series of events. Event trees start from an *initiating event* and are typically drawn from left to right with the causal events (called *top events*) listed as questions at top of the diagram. At each top event, the path divides into two or more branches depending on the outcome of the top event with the straight or up branch representing success and the down branch representing failure. Each unique path through the event tree defines a *scenario* and the conditions resulting from the

occurrence of the events in the scenario is called an *end state*. End states are potentially unique but in practice a limited number of end state categories are defined and used for collecting results. The exhibit below shows a simple event tree. The numbers in this example are shown using scientific notation which is very handy for expressing very large or very small numbers. For example, 6.9E-03 is shorthand for 0.0069.

Exhibit 7-13 Example Event Tree

Primary Shell Breach Initiating Event	Secondary Shell Integrity OK	Annulus Vent Integrity OK	Leak Size is Small?	Seq. #	Frequency per Year	End State
DSTSB	SSI	AVI	SIZE			
1.28E-01	9.16E-01	9.41E-01	N/I	1	1.1E-01	SUCCESS
		5.88E-02	N/I	2	6.9E-03	BPL
	8.42E-02	N/I	0.00	3	0.0E+00	SLK
			1.00	4	1.1E-02	LLKDST

Legend:
N/I = Not Important

The event tree quantification process begins with an initiating event frequency which can be an actual frequency (events/unit of time) or can be 1.0. If the initiating event is a frequency then the scenario results will also be frequencies that sum to the frequency of the initiator. When the initiator is set to 1.0, then the scenario results will be conditional probabilities that sum to 1.0. In either case, the values assigned at each branch point to the down branch are called *split fractions* (SF) and the values used for the straight branch are complements (1-SF). The split fractions are conditional probabilities and are conditional, or dependent, on the occurrence of the initiator and all the top events that precede the split fraction in the event tree structure. It is this explicit specification of dependencies that makes event tree analysis so powerful, but also potentially complicated. I will return to this subject in Chapter 12. Event trees also appear in other specialized forms, such as decision trees, but I will discuss them only in their general form.

Fault Trees

As stated earlier, fault trees are the most common deductive modeling tool. They are constructed by first specifying an unwanted event or condition called the top event (again) and then all possible causes leading to the top event are specified using a disciplined structure consisting of basic events (requiring no further development) and intermediate events (requiring further development) linked together by logic gates. Although there are a fair variety of gate types available for use in complex fault trees, by far the two most commonly used are the OR gate (true if any input is true) and the AND gate (true only if all inputs are true). The Exhibit below shows a simple fault tree.

Exhibit 7-14   Example Fault Tree

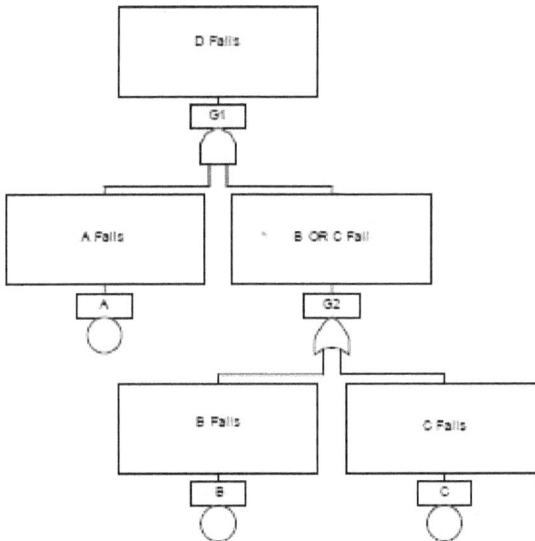

Source: NASA Fault Tree Handbook with Aerospace Applications

The best source document describing basic fault tree methodology is the Fault Tree Handbook[5] published by the U.S. Nuclear Regulatory Commission but be advised that

---

[5] Fault Tree Handbook, NUREG-0492, U.S. Nuclear Regulatory Commission, January 1981.

solution methods and computer codes have advance far beyond the material presented in the handbook.

System Simulations

The risk assessment modeling methods we have reviewed thus far all predict the behavior of a system by estimating the individual performance of system elements that make up the system. The simulation is processed sequentially using data inputs to characterize system element behavior and logical and mathematical rules to define the relationships of the system elements to each. Although time may be a performance metric in the calculation the simulation elements are processed in a sequential order defined by the modeler. Models of this type are called discrete event simulations or *Monte Carlo simulations* because the data inputs are typically selected at random from a distribution of possible values input by the modeler. The fundamentals of this modeling approach were first formalized at Los Alamos National Laboratory during and just after the Manhattan Project by John von Newman, Stanislaw Ulam, Enrico Fermi, and others.[6]

Another method for system simulation uses differential equations to define the elements of the system and calculates their status simultaneously at regularly defined time intervals. This modeling method is called *dynamic simulation* and includes examples such as global climate and electric grid models. The actual run time of a dynamic simulation is determined by the size and complexity of the model and the processing power of the computer performing the calculation. Dynamic simulations are most commonly used to model complex physical systems. A number of software environments have been developed to facilitate dynamic simulation but they require significant user skill to operate. Also, because they solve differential equations using complex numerical methods, the results can go non-linear and blow up in ways that may or may not reflect real world physics.

---

[6] *The Beginning of the Monte Carlo Method*, Metropolis, Nicholas, Los Alamos Science, 1987.

Solving Real Problems

In practice, a competent risk analyst may use all of the methods and tools I have discussed here and more to assess a large complex system. For example, an event tree model for an initiating event may use fault trees to answer some top event questions while others are answered with system simulations. At an even higher level, one performance metric could be assessed with an integrated event tree/fault tree risk model like I just described, while another metric is assessed with a Monte Carlo simulation. The details behind how a large risk model is nailed together can be quite complicated. The exhibit below presents a flow diagram illustrating the quantification process for a large risk model.

Exhibit 7-15 Risk Model Quantification Process Example

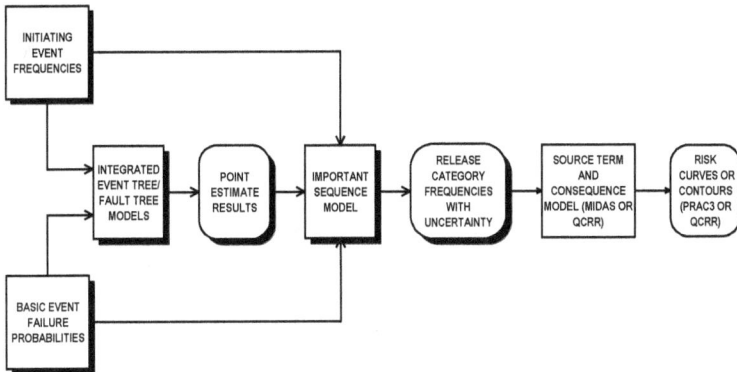

At this point I hope that the taste I have presented here of scenario modeling has led you to the conclusion that it is an involved process that requires skill and experience to perform well. I will return to discuss important aspects of the risk modeling process as we proceed but for now, I'll call a truce.

Identify Initiators and Build ESD's

So how can the initiating events be found? And, how can we ever be sure the list is adequately complete? Ah ha, you have just discovered what may be the best reason of all for doing a qualitative risk assessment. In addition to the direct benefits of finding and mitigating "low fruit" risk issues, qualitative risk assessments generate a quite comprehensive list of potential initiating events. In fact, if you don't have a qualitative risk assessment, you will need to do something similar to search out and identify initiators to start the quantitative analysis.

But regardless of how candidate initiating events are identified, they need to be organized and consolidated before proceeding with scenario analysis and quantification. To accomplish this, a modeling tool called a *master logic diagram* (MLD) is used. A MLD is a logic diagram that resembles a fault tree but without the formal mathematical properties. MLDs are typically constructed from the top down and begin with an unwanted condition called the "top event" which is the opposite of success. The first level of blocks under the top event specifies the conditions that must exist to cause the top event. The second and subsequent levels then subdivide the possible pathways to the top event into more specific causes. Initiating events then feed into one or more of the blocks at the bottom of the MLD. This exercise serves two important functions. First, if the MLD is logically complete, that is the top event can only be caused by satisfying one of the logical pathways through the MLD, then the results of the risk assessment to follow are also logically complete. This is not to say that we have (or ever can) identify all possible pathways (scenarios) from initiator to top event. But having identified all possible paths through at least one level of the MLD we can now say that all possible scenarios must go through a known MLD path. This statement now shifts the question of completeness from the logic of the risk model to the frequency that will be assessed for each MLD pathway. Closure on the question of frequency will then be achieved by the explicit calculation of uncertainty.

The second important function of the MLD is to help organize and quantify the initiating event list. If we matrix a list of potential initiators against the bottom events of the MLD and indicate each initiator that could cause each MLD bottom event, a distinct pattern will form for each row of the matrix showing how each potential initiator impacts on the MLD. This pattern in each row is called an *impact vector* because a potential initiator may impact only one or several MLD basic events. The patterns formed by the impact vectors give us a way to organize the initiating event list. Potential initiators that display the same impact vector are candidates to have their frequencies combined for further analysis because they impact the MLD in the same way whereas potential initiators with unique impact vectors will require individual attention in the remaining analysis.

The following two Exhibits show an example MLD and an example of the initiating event organization process.

Exhibit 7-16 Example Master Logic Diagram[7]

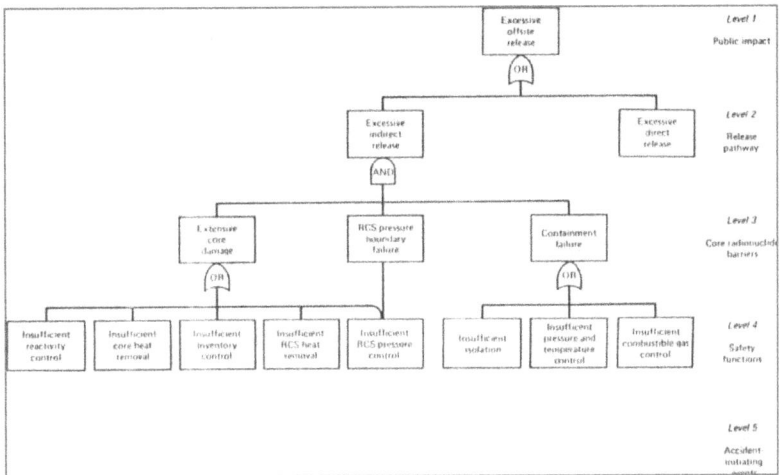

[7] MLD from the *Midland Nuclear Plant Probabilistic Risk Assessment*, Consumers Power Company, Jackson, Michigan, 1984

Exhibit 7-17   Example Initiator - MLD Matrix with Impact Vectors

Initiator		PHA Scenario	MLD BASIC EVENTS															
			Retrieval Tank Vent Drain Leak	Slurry Transfer Line Leak	Slurry Transfer Pit Leak	Retrieval Tank Leak	Retrieval Tank Waste Ejection to Atmosphere	Retrieval Tank Overflow	Retrieval Conveyance System Leak	Supernatant Transfer Line Leak	Supernatant Transfer Pit Leak	Receiver Tank Leak	Receiver Tank Waste Ejection to Atmosphere	Receiver Tank Overflow	Retrieval Tank Unfiltered Dome Space Release	Receiver Tank Unfiltered Dome Space Release	Retrieval Tank HEPA Filter Breach	Receiver Tank HEPA Filter Breach
Code	#	Description	1	2	3	4	5	6	7	8	9	10	11	12	13	14	15	16
CNVLK	A3A-3	Leak/breach of the air conveyance system module (ACM)													X			
CRIT	SG-3 AG-3	Criticality in tank										X						
DRLK	SG-8	Misrouting of vent filter backwash	X															
DRLK	SG-7	Vent drain system leak	X															
FB1	S3A-6	Vent filter breach in retrieval tank													X	X	X	X
FB1/2	SG-5 AG-5	High wind damage to vent system													X	X		
HILVL1	S2A-1	Excessive water addition to retrieval tank				X		X						X				
LNLK	S3A-1 A3A-4	Seismic event, transfer line leak without shutdown switch failure		X						X	X							
LNLK	S3A-2 A3A-5	Seismic event, transfer line leak with shutdown switch operation		X						X	X							

Chapter 8 DATA, UNCERTAINTY AND ARITHMETIC

Exhibit 7-15 showed an example of the quantification process used for a large, complex risk model. In this example, all the risk modeling methods and tools we have discussed so far fall into the box labeled "integrated event tree/fault tree model". In this chapter we will take a peek at the other steps needed to get from the risk model to results, and then we will look at results in more detail in the next chapter.

Likelihood Data

The first steps we see in the risk quantification process flow chart indicate that initiating event and basic event data is needed as an input to the logic model. As I indicated earlier, what we are talking about here is *frequency type data* that is mathematically expressed as:

$$Frequency\ or\ Probability = \frac{A\ Number\ of\ Events}{Units\ of\ Time\ or\ a\ Number\ of\ Trials}$$

The answers to the second of our three fundamental risk questions, likelihood, can come in several formats. In *quantitative risk assessments*, likelihood can be expressed as a *frequency*, that is the number of events observed in a measured number of trials (N/T) or as the number of events observed per unit of time (e.g. deaths per year). There are also situations where it is useful to set the initiating event frequency equal to 1.0 and then have the end state results be *conditional probabilities* with values between zero and 1.0.

OK, but where can this type of data be found? The philosophical answer is everywhere and nowhere. Useful data on all sorts of issues is all around us, and yet it is never totally complete or completely relevant. Assembling the best available data to an important prediction of the future is both a science and an art requiring extensive skill and experience. My goal in this chapter is once again to help you appreciate what expert analysts can do and know how to use their expertise to your benefit.

First, a comprehensive dissertation on probability and statistics is outside the scope of this book and beyond my capabilities. However, this is a subject where what you don't know can hurt you, so I am going to address some important topics that are sometimes not covered well in more academic texts.

Probability Distribution Basics

Because our knowledge of event likelihood is incomplete, we will describe our state of knowledge of the events with probability distributions. These come in two basic types. A *discrete distribution* is one where the variable under study can only take on certain specific values (e.g. heads or tails). A *continuous distribution* is one where the variable can take on any value between the specified low and high limits and this type of distribution will be the general focus for the rest of this section.

The example below shows the same continuous distribution presented in two forms. The first exhibit shows the density function format and the second shows the cumulative format. The density function represents the rate of change or first derivative of the cumulative distribution.

Exhibit 8-1 Example Probability Density Distribution

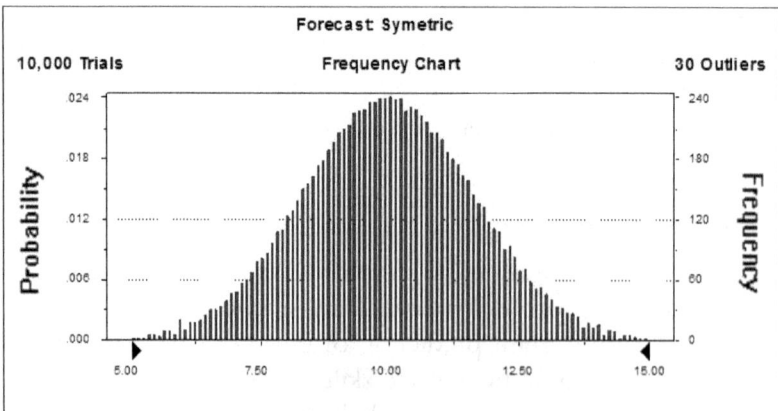

Exhibit 8-2 Example Cumulative Probability Distribution

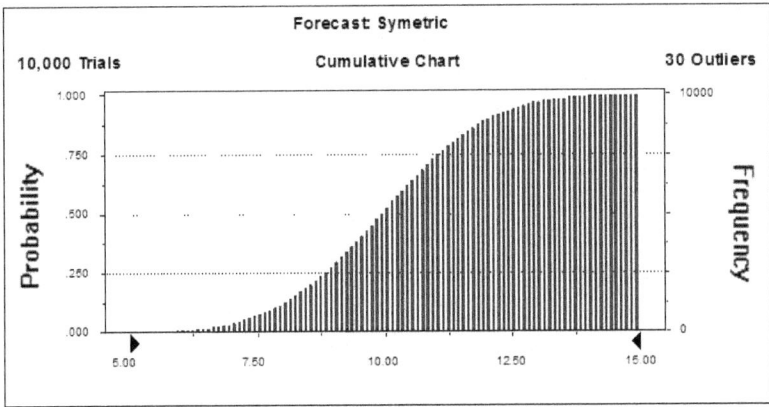

The next exhibit shows a density function with its commonly used central tendency parameters the mean, median, and mode. These parameters fall to the same value for a symmetric distribution like the one shown above. But for a skewed distribution like the one shown below, they take on quite different values. This is important because these parameters are often used in simple arithmetic calculations to represent the entire distribution. The breadth of the distribution can be described with percentile values or with statistical parameters known as the standard deviation or variance.

Exhibit 8-3 Example Skewed Probability Distribution

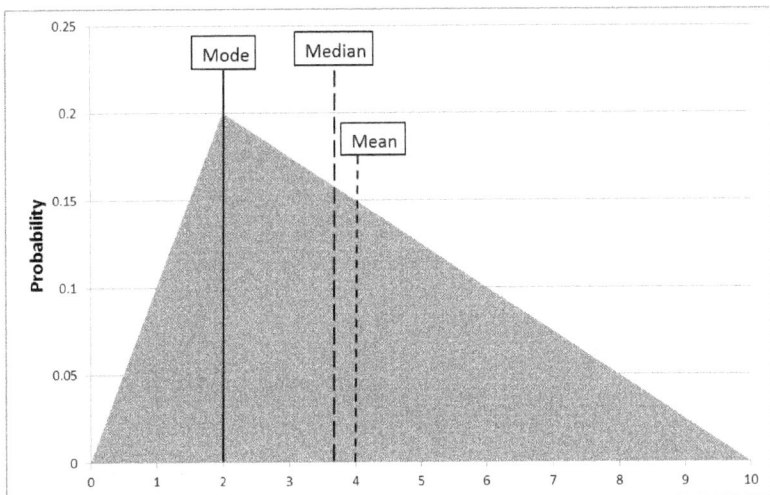

Building a Distribution

The construction of a probability distribution from actual data is done by plotting the frequency of all data points to form a histogram like the example shown below.

Exhibit 8-4 Histogram of Data

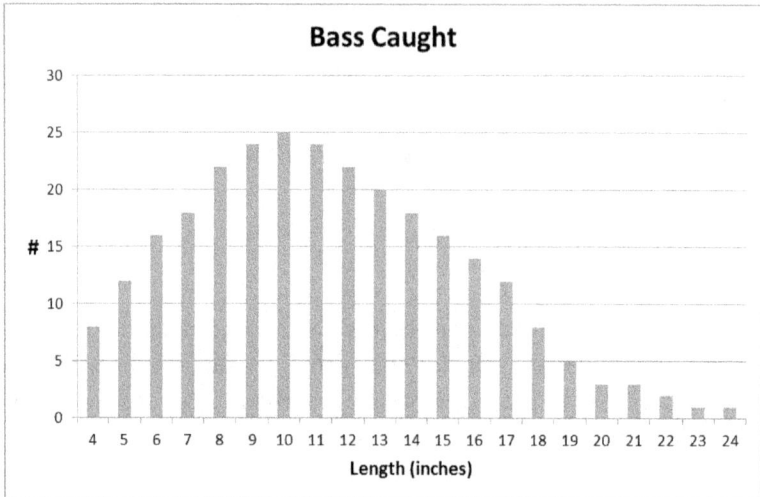

Next, if the frequencies in the histogram are transformed into relative frequencies and normalized to 1.0, an empirical probability distribution is formed that exhibits the same general shape as the histogram.

Exhibit 8-5   Probability Distribution Created From Histogram Data

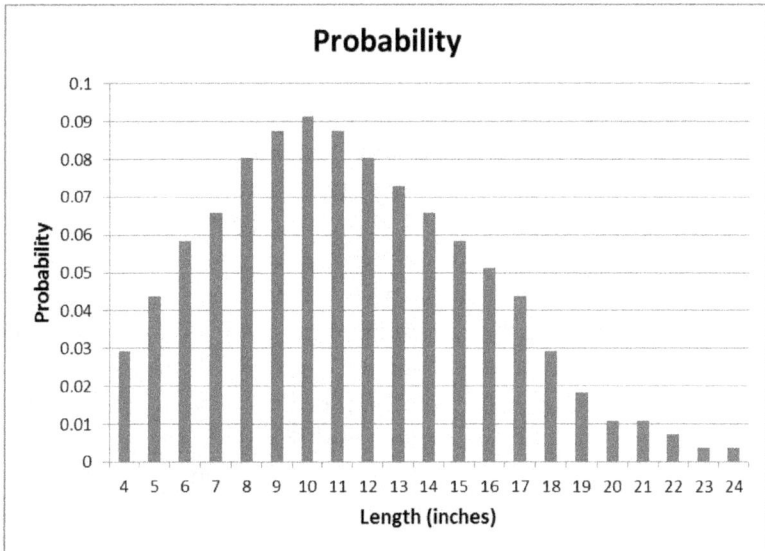

If the data used to build a distribution in this manner is relevant to the problem and robust enough to define the extremities of the distribution well, you're done!   Any central tendency parameters or percentile values that are needed can be directly calculated using the compiled data. More commonly, however, the data set is not robust or completely relevant. In these cases, the incomplete information can be represented by selecting an analytical distribution form to describe the distribution. Normal, lognormal, triangular, and exponential are examples of the more common analytical forms commonly used. There are quite a few more available for use, however. To build a distribution using one of these analytical forms you must supply at least the minimal information needed to create them mathematically, which is some combination of the mean and standard deviation or percentiles. Another approach that can be used is to fit an analytical form to a data set. This is very easily done now via computer with readily available statistics codes. You merely enter the available data into the code and it automatically tests the statistical goodness of fit for each of a library of stored analytical forms and reports the results for your selection.

Alas, the preceding paragraphs are far from a complete discussion of this subject. In quantitative risk assessment, probability is a subjective notion and is based on all the evidence available to the risk analyst including reasoned thinking as well as data. Unfortunately, this usage of the word "probability" conflicts with the way statisticians use it. In statistics, probability or confidence refers to the degree to which a sample of data points taken from a larger population accurately represents that larger population. You can hear this use of probability almost daily in opinion poll results where it is referred to as the "margin of error". This philosophical difference between subjectivists and frequentists may sound like a fine academic point, but it can be the source of significant confusion and miscommunication. Strict frequintists (statisticians) believe that probability distributions can only be developed from statistically significant frequency type data whereas subjectivists (risk analysts) treat probability as a state of knowledge that can come from reasoned thinking as well as data. You may not sense a significant issue in this difference, but among data experts in statistics and risk analysis, these are fight'n words.

The mathematical basis for the use of reasoned thinking in assessing probability is defined by Bayes Theorem. Because of this, subjectivists are also called Bayesians. Mathematical discussions of Bayes Theorem and its uses can be found in many academic texts, but I recommend the Kaplan and Garrick paper I referenced earlier most highly as a start. For a more holistic description of how the human mind actually processes information using Bayesian reasoning rather than formal mathematics, however, I highly recommend *Thinking Fast and Slow*, by Daniel Kahneman[8]. Kahneman, a psychologist, has done extensive research on how the human mind processes information and makes decisions, both right and wrong. In this

---

[8] *Thinking Fast and Slow*, Kahneman, Daniel, Farrar, Straus and Giroux, 2011

book he uses research results to describe subjective reasoning long before he explicitly mentions Bayes Theorem.

I'll try to be careful in my use of the words probability and frequency in this book and you should be alert to the way they are used in any risk information that is important to you. Again, if you would like to dig deeper into this subject, the Kaplan & Garrick paper discussed earlier provides a much more robust discussion of this issue.

Combining Distributions

Now that we have an understanding of what probability distributions are and how they can be built, we need to address some issues about how to combine them properly that if not understood, can lead to serious errors in results. By "combine" I am referring to the seeming simple mathematical operations of addition/subtraction and multiplication/division. But when uncertainty is involved, things aren't quite so simple. First, let's talk about what it takes to really do it right. For small problems that use analytic distributions to describe uncertainty, the combination can be done analytically. In other words, from the equations that represent each base distribution, a new equation can be derived that represents the combination of the two originals. However, this approach isn't practical for large problems or non-analytical distributions built from real data. This situation represented a real roadblock to the use of statistical analysis for many problems until a team of scientists at Los Alamos National Laboratory led by John von Newman, Stanislaw Ulam, Enrico Fermi, and others developed what they called the Monte Carlo method.[9] What the Los Alamos team accomplished was the marriage of statistical sampling with the newly invented electronic computer. What Monte Carlo analysis (named for the favorite gambling spot of Ulam's uncle) does is randomly select data points from each base distribution, combine them as instructed, and then build the resulting distribution for the combined value. Although still

---

[9] *The Beginning of the Monte Carlo Method*, Metropolis, Nicholas, Los Alamos Science, 1987.

cumbersome and expensive at the time of its creation in the 1940s, subsequent advances in computing power have brought Monte Carlo analysis capability within the reach of anyone with a personal computer.

Although widely available, most quantitative risk analyses are still not performed with the Monte Carlo method. Whether because of lack of knowledge, limited resources, or just laziness, most risk analyses are performed using some sort of representative point estimate values, that is a single number chosen to represent a parameter that is, in truth, uncertain. This can lead to serious errors in analysis results. This is because the only point value of a distribution that can be used in combinatorial arithmetic to get the right answer is the arithmetic mean value of the distribution. If you think about this intuitively for a moment, since the mean is the average of all the data points in the distribution, using any other value to represent the distribution must be wrong. It is. However, in countless cases, people select "conservative" point values often far away from the mean to represent an unknown parameter and eagerly combine many such point values to produce a supposedly "conservative" result. Even when uncertainties are not high, the result can be not just overly conservative but plain wrong. Exhibit 8-6 shows the Monte Carlo result for the addition of four independent distributions (we'll talk more about that later), all of which have a mean value of 6.0 and a 90 percentile value of 7.575. The red line represents the mean of the sum of the four distributions calculated using the Monte Carlo method (24) while the green line represents the sum of conservative (90%) point estimate values for each parameter (about 30.3). The magnitude of the error in the result for this simple example is about 26%. For real world size problems, this type of error can make point value results completely useless. So remember, when combining point estimate values, only use *mean* values!

Exhibit 8-6 Error Induced by Point Value Summation

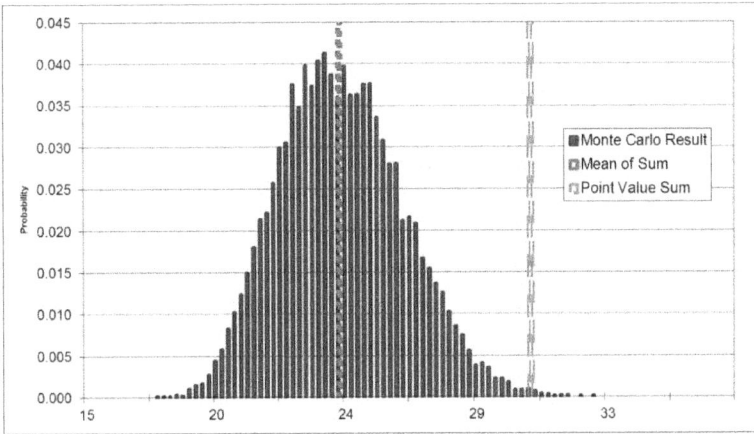

Consequence Data

So far in this chapter the discussion has focused on likelihood type data. But to calculate risk we will also need to quantify, with uncertainty, consequences. Typical consequence metrics include human fatalities, injuries, or other health effects, and damages as measured in dollars or other units. Consequences estimates are conditional, that is they only occur if the risk scenario takes place. Thus the arithmetic of the risk calculation and the units used to express risk look like the following equations.

$$\text{Frequency} \times \text{Consequence} = \text{Risk}$$

$$\frac{events}{unit\ of\ time} * \frac{consequences}{event} = \frac{consequences}{unit\ of\ time}$$

The discussion above about probability distributions still applies but now the focus is on quantifying the potential consequences per event.

Chapter 9 - USING RISK ASSESSMENT RESULTS

Here in Part II, I have laid out a lot of information about risk analysis concepts, methods, and tools very quickly and showed some examples of results along the way. As indicated earlier, however, this book is not intended to provide a comprehensive "how-to" guide for risk analysis. There is much more that I have not presented. When it comes to results, though, you will need a reasonably complete understanding of what they can look like and how to use them to your maximum advantage. It is time then to survey the different formats results can come in and discuss what they can tell us about risk.

Risk Analysis Result Formats

The first division of risk analysis methods we discussed was qualitative verses quantitative analysis. Qualitative analysis results can vary from simple pair wise rankings (A>B) to scenario lists that have estimates of likelihood and consequence ranges or bins. Although qualitative analysis can provide many useful insights, remember that qualitative results are fundamentally judgmental rankings made against some benchmark event. They should not be stretched to provide a basis for cost/benefit decisions or risk goal compliance.

Quantitative risk analysis results, in contrast, produce a numeric estimate of performance on one or more metric scales. As discussed earlier, this type of result can be used to provide a basis to support cost/benefit decision making and risk goal compliance. But before we can discuss how this is done, we need a good foundation of knowledge about the formats they can come in and the information they contain. This is summarized in the table on the next page.

Exhibit 9-1 Summary of Quantitative Risk Analysis Result Formats

Analysis Type	Uncertainty Included?	
	No	Yes
Mission Analysis	(I) Single Point Estimate *(Exhibit 8-1)*	(II) Probability Distribution in Density or Cumulative Form *(Exhibits 7-12 & 8-1)*
Continuous Process Analysis	(III) Risk Curve in Frequency Format *(Exhibit 7-11)*	(IV) Risk Curve in Probability of Frequency Format *(Exhibit 9-2)*

The first of the four possible result formats, the single point estimate is a very straightforward numeric value for the event under study. The second format, the probability distribution adds the explicit expression of our state of knowledge regarding uncertainty in the single point estimate and examples were presented in Exhibits 7-12 and 8-1. These first two formats are used for the mission type analyses discussed in Chapter 7. The final two formats are used for continuous or production type systems where results are calculated as a function of time. Format three, the risk curve in frequency format, was shown earlier in Chapter 7 but did not include uncertainty. To include uncertainty, we now we introduce the final and most robust form for risk results, the probability of frequency format shown in Exhibit 9-2. If you followed my earlier suggestion to study the Kaplan & Garrick paper, you are already familiar with this picture. Since this is the most comprehensive form for quantitative risk analysis results, we will use this format to discuss how to read and use results. Once you understand probability of frequency results, you will recognize the other formats as special cases derived from this format and be comfortable using any of them.

Exhibit 9-2   Risk Curve in Probability of Frequency Format

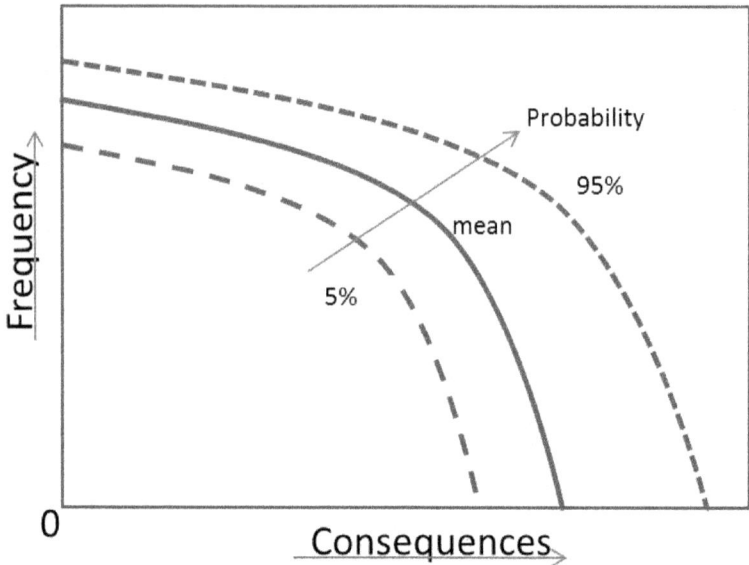

First, let's talk about the general form of the results. The generic risk results shown in the Exhibit are drawn in two dimensions with probability shown as increasing from lower left to upper right. But probability is really a third axis rising vertically from the page. The true picture is then three dimensional with probability causing the results to be shaped like a mountain range sweeping from upper left to lower right. The peak or spine of the mountain range follows the mean risk curve while the decreasing foothills are described by the percentile curves falling off left and right of the mean. Also, the height of the probability "mountain" generally falls off and the base becomes wider as we follow the results from upper left to lower right. This is because the uncertainty around low frequency, high consequence events is generally greater than that for high frequency, low consequence events.

If you pick any point on the consequence axis and plot the probabilities along a vertical line or slice upward, you will get a probability density function of the frequencies for that consequence level. As you move from left to right along the consequence axis, these probability slices generally become lower and broader.

For type III and IV risk results, another common and useful result is the expected value of the loss or damage. This is obtained by the convolution of the scenario frequencies and consequences and is expressed in units of loss or damage per unit time for the analysis (\$/year or deaths/year). For a type III risk result, the expected value will be a point value and, for a type IV risk result, a probability distribution.

By calculating the expected value of the loss or damage before and after the implementation of risk reduction actions, we can assess the loss or damage avoided by adoption of the risk reduction actions and compare this with the expected costs to judge their value.

Identifying Contributors

Now, with a basic picture of what a risk analysis result looks like, let's examine what information they contain and how to use them. Real world risk curves are developed by plotting many (thousands to millions) individual scenario results from a Monte Carlo analysis. A useful risk model is structured using methods and tools like those reviewed in Chapter 7 so that not only is a result produced, but so that the contributing initiators and intermediate conditional failure events are also remembered for each individual scenario. With this capability, results for any given level of consequence can be decomposed to reveal the contributing events. Using this knowledge, the risk analyst can identify potential actions that could change the bottom line risk results. This is the real reason for doing quantitative risk analysis.

Monte Carlo analysis codes also generally include the capability to calculate the contribution each input distribution makes to the uncertainty in a combined result. This is called sensitivity analysis and it identifies and ranks the input parameters that need to be changed, if the preliminary results are not acceptable (see Chapter 6). The exhibit below presents an actual example of this type of result.

Exhibit 9-3 Probability Curve with Sensitivity Results

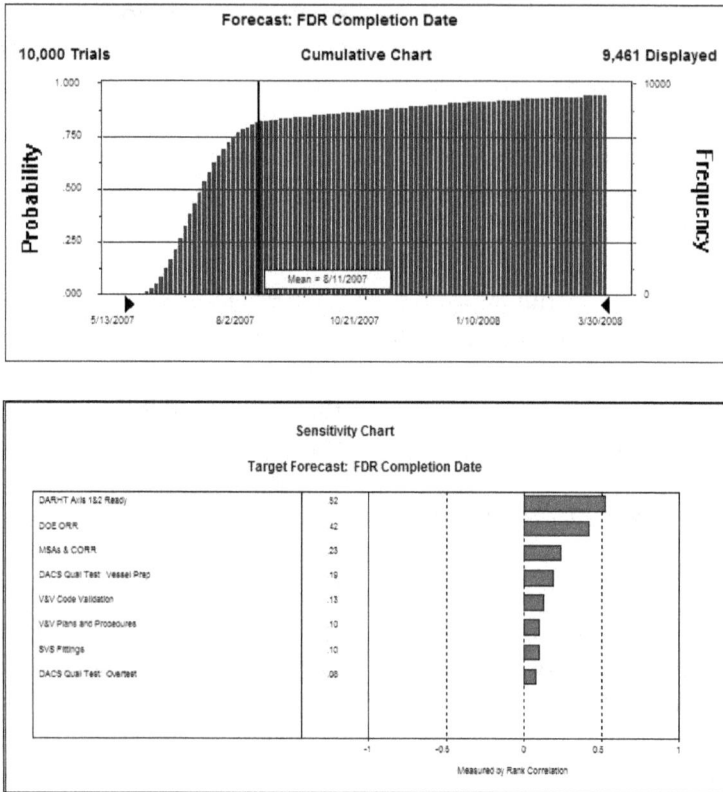

Risk models developed with logic modeling tools like event trees and fault trees, provide additional capabilities to identify and rank the contribution of both base inputs and intermediate events to the final results. These are called "importance" measures and are extremely powerful diagnostic tools for risk management. The next exhibit presents an example of how importance measures were used to identify the leading contributors to risk and point the way to improved system performance and lower risk. This example provides the basis for my repeated claims that quantitative risk analysis provides a basis to support cost/benefit decision making and risk goal compliance

Exhibit 9-4 Importance Measures for Mean Risk Results

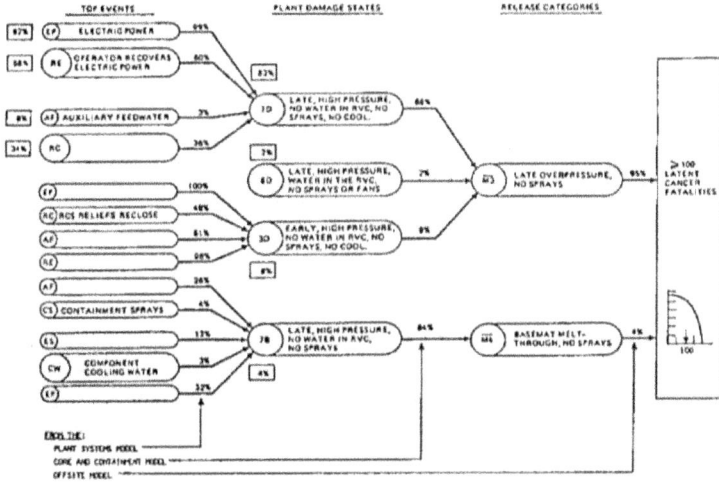

Another important aspect of reading results comes from the risk curves themselves. Exhibit 9-5 shows a risk curve in frequency format and includes the major scenarios that contribute to risk as identified from importance calculations.

Exhibit 9-5 Risk Curve Showing Contributing Scenarios

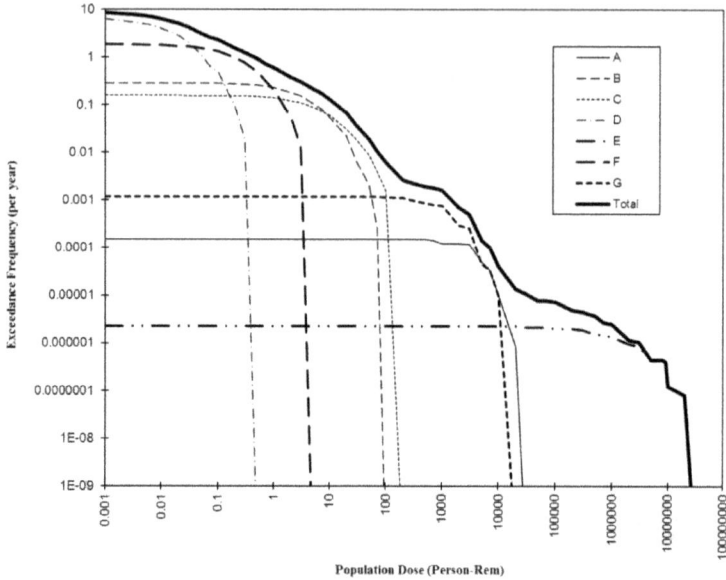

Population Dose (Person-Rem)

The total risk curve is the sum of the risk curves for the individual scenarios (all scenarios are not shown). Notice that different regions of the total risk curve are controlled by different underlying scenarios. For example for the high frequency-low consequence region, scenarios D and F control the total while the low frequency-high consequence region at the other end is controlled by scenario E. This capability to identify contributors to different regions of the total risk curve will be important to our discussion in the next section.

Determining Risk Acceptability

Our risk management process flowchart shown in Chapter 6 contains a decision block where we ask if the assessed risk is acceptable. With risk assessment results like the examples we have shown here and the ability to decompose those results to identify the underlying contributors, we are now ready to answer that question.

There are two basic approaches that can be taken to answer the risk acceptability question. They are benefit/cost analysis and

94

risk goal setting. In its simplest form, traditional benefit/cost analysis is performed by comparing the estimated gain or profit anticipated for a proposed initiative with the estimated cost of executing that action. If the anticipated benefit is greater than the estimated cost, then a "rational" actor would chose to proceed and demur if the projected costs exceed the benefit. But using the information available from quantitative risk analysis results, we can now answer the acceptability question with much greater precision and confidence (pun intended).

First, we can use a type I risk result to determine if the expected value of the anticipated benefits of an enterprise is greater than the expected value of the estimated costs? Alternatively, we can evaluate the uncertainty in both the projected benefits and costs and compile a type II risk analysis predicting the probability of the net benefit. By adding consideration of the timing of planned events, we can also plot the results of the analysis in cumulative form to predict when break-even will be achieved. Example results from this type of analysis are shown below.

Exhibit 9-6   Risk Results for New Venture Break Even Time (green line)

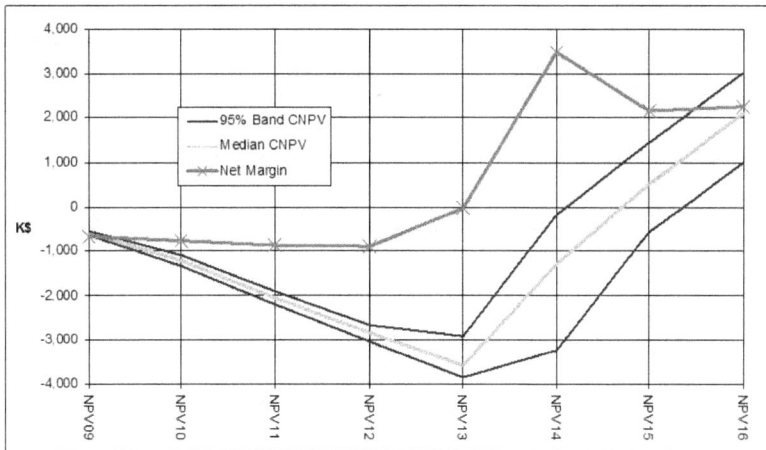

I hope this brief introduction has impressed you with the power of benefit/cost analysis and, we will have more to say on this subject shortly. But first let's digress a bit and look at how risk goals can also be used to answer the acceptability question. Risk goals are sometimes recommended by industry standards or required by regulatory authorities. They can also be used in situations where benefit/cost analysis may not be complete because some consequences may be hard to measure or in cases where a decision maker's values are not represented fully by financial analysis. We'll discuss how to account for these issues later, but for now let's just look conceptually at how risk results can be used to measure compliance with risk goals. To illustrate this process I have taken a type III risk result showing a mean risk curve and overlaid on it three different types of risk goals.

Exhibit 9-7 Risk Goals Illustration

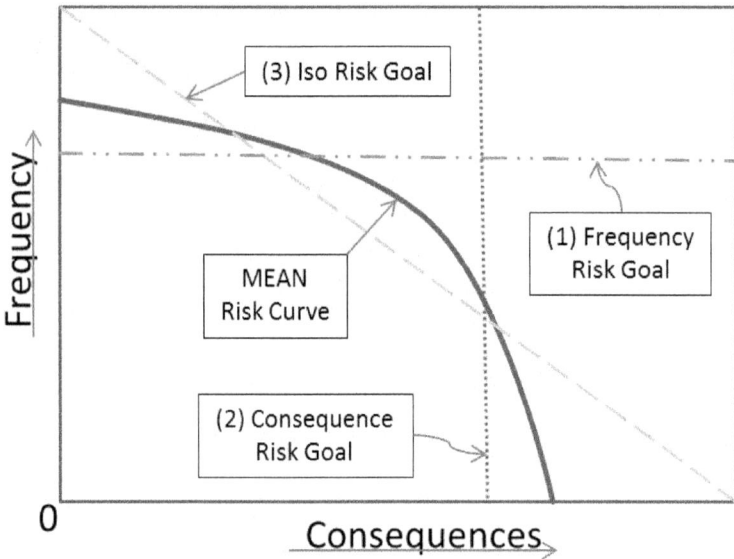

The dot and dash line (1) represents a frequency risk goal. This can be used where a specified event or consequence should not be observed above the level indicated by the dot and dash line (1). To meet this goal, scenarios from the risk analysis results that cause the mean risk curve to rise above this line must be identified and eliminated or reduced in likelihood.

The second illustrated risk goal (2) is a consequence goal. This can be used where it is desired to limit the magnitude of consequence that can occur. To meet this goal, scenarios from the risk analysis results that cause the mean risk curve to extend beyond the dotted line must be identified and eliminated or reduced in magnitude of loss or damage.

Lastly, the third illustrated risk goal (3) is an iso-risk goal. In this example, the dashed line represents a constant level of risk where the product of the frequency and consequence is equal at all points. The actual shape of this line will vary depending on the scaling of the frequency and consequence axes. This type of goal can be used where it is desired to limit the overall risk from a specified hazard at any frequency or consequence level to less than a specified risk value. To meet this goal, scenarios from the risk analysis results that cause the mean risk curve to extend beyond the dashed line at any point must be identified and eliminated or reduced in frequency or magnitude.

Another common feature of risk goals is the use of layered or progressive action levels. Exhibit 9-8 illustrates an iso-risk goal with two levels. The lower threshold level indicated by the dashed line and labeled ALERT could trigger the initiation of an effort to identify and mitigate the scenarios pushing the mean risk curve across this line while planned activities continue. If the mean risk curve had extended beyond the DANGER level represented by the dotted line, however, that result might require a halt of planned activities until the scenarios of concern can be identified and mitigated.

Exhibit 9-8 Alert & Danger Risk Goals

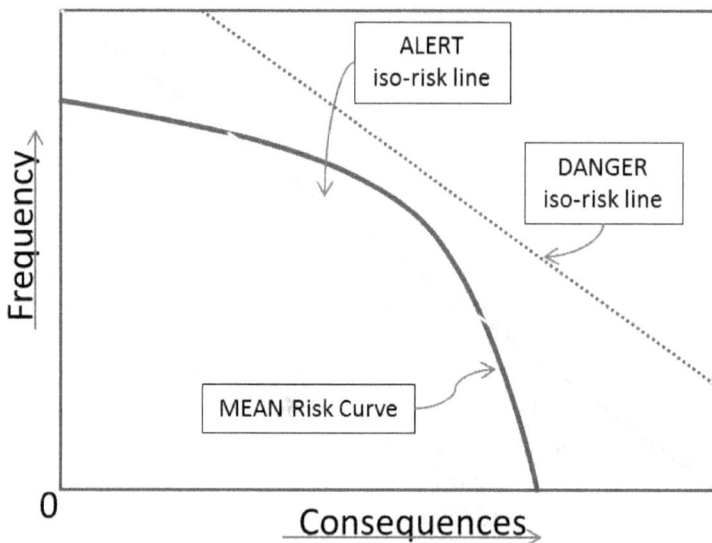

Risk Reduction Actions

Whether or not acceptability has been achieved, quantitative risk analysis results can also allow us to "turn up the microscope" to identify potential actions that could increase benefits or decrease costs in any original or baseline action plan. To do this, we will ask the acceptance question a little differently. From a quantitative risk analysis, we can ask what risk reduction actions (RRAs) would produce the greatest benefit measured by the loss or damage *avoided* by successful implementation of any proposed risk reduction action.

To determine benefit in this way, we need comprehensive risk analysis results of the type described in the previous section and we need to calculate risk results both before and after any proposed risk reduction actions being considered for implementation. From the before and after risk results we can determine the loss or damage that would be avoided by completion of the risk reduction action. The estimated cost of implementing the proposed risk reduction action then becomes the second element in the analysis, allowing the net magnitude or benefit/cost ratio to be determined. Sensitivity and importance calculations provide the loss or damage avoided results needed for this determination. They accomplish this by identifying the scenarios and events that contribute the most to the calculated risk as shown earlier in this chapter. Once the important scenarios and events are known, the changes needed to reduce their likelihood of occurrence and/or consequences can be developed as shown way back in our risk management process flowchart.

Developing risk reduction actions for consideration is, of course, highly specific to the activity under study and generally the responsibility of SME's, not the risk analyst. However, a protocol of sorts for performing this task has evolved around the use of four RRA tactics that can be used to organize RRA development. They are[10]:

Avoidance – This tactic seeks to eliminate the source of the uncertainty. This is generally accomplished through a fundamental change in requirements or specifications. An example would be to move a facility vulnerable to earthquake damage away from areas of high seismicity. Avoidance actions should only be taken after a thorough evaluation of the potential impacts on mission and/or functional capabilities has been made.

Transfer – Transfer tactics involve the reallocation of risk from one party to another. Transfer strategies are generally financial arrangements that require the payment of a risk premium to accomplish the transfer. Examples include fixed price contracts and insurance arrangements such as a performance bond. Care needs to be exercised in making risk transfer agreements to be sure the insuring party can fulfill their obligations when needed. Failure of risk transfer arrangements was a major factor in the great recession.

---

[10] I cannot cite the definitive origin of these strategies for RRA development but I first encountered it in the *Risk Management Guide for DoD Acquisition* which first came out about 1998 and I have seen it copied in many other places, always without attribution.

Control – Risk control tactics seek to reduce the likelihood of occurrence of the risk event and/or mitigate its consequences, should it occur. This is generally the broadest and most varied strategy. Categories of control strategies include trade studies and modeling/simulation of system designs, targeted research and development programs, competing alternative designs, phased development programs, and early system tests or demonstrations.

Acceptance – Risk acceptance is an appropriate tactic for risks that remain after application of the first three strategies and for low-level risks where formal response actions would not be cost effective. The most universally used risk acceptance strategy involves the establishment of reserves or contingencies for time, funds or other resources. These reserves can be allocated to specifically identified risks or held as true reserves for unknown problems.

A more sophisticated method for applying these tactics in RRA development employs the risk curves and goals just introduced. The following exhibit illustrates this method graphically. As can be seen, the activity specific risk results are used to apply each RRA tactic in a region in the risk profile where it is most effective to produce an overall RRA strategy that is risk informed. First, the avoidance and transfer tactics are used to mitigate unacceptably high consequences. Then control type RRAs are deployed to address undesirable but manageable risks. Finally, acceptance tactics are used to mitigate the remaining low risk issues.

Exhibit 9-9 Risk Informed RRA Strategy

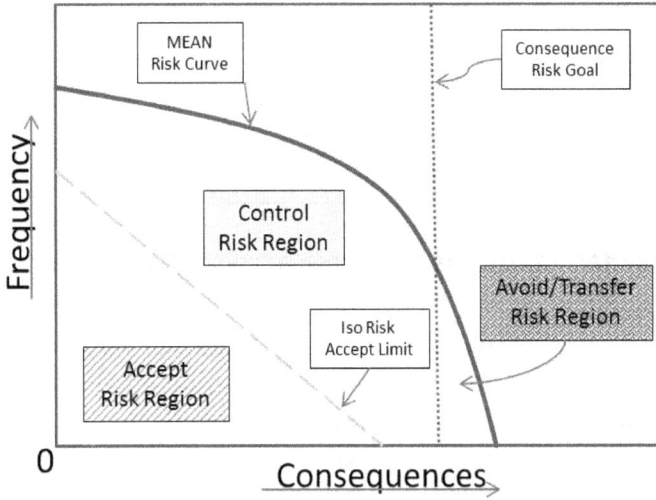

Part III – How Risk Management Can Fail (and How to Spot the Danger Signs)

> *You don't have to know how to cook a steak*
> *to tell when it's burnt.*

Chapter 10 - REASONS RISK MANAGEMENT CAN FAIL

In Part I, I systematically applied four questions to reveal how risk management failed to prevent three of the more spectacular catastrophes of our time. In Part II, I then gave a brief overview of available risk management concepts and methods and presented examples of what real risk analysis results look like and how they can be used to manage risk. Part II was done, as I stated earlier, not to be a comprehensive guide for performing risk management or risk analysis, but to establish a basic understanding of the process and a common language for use in the balance of the book. With that in mind, we are now going to use some of the concepts and methods from Part II to show where those four questions in Part I came from and how you can use them to critically evaluate your own issues of interest without being an expert risk analyst.

To do this I am going to reach back to the discussion of the master logic diagram (MLD) in Chapter 7. As stated earlier, a MLD is a logic diagram that resembles a fault tree but without the formal mathematical properties. A MLD can be used to identify the logical pathways through which scenarios must travel to result in the unwanted event or condition described at the top of the MLD. So let's use a MLD to examine the question of risk management failure. The result is shown in the following Exhibit.

102

Exhibit 10-1   Level 2 Master Logic Diagram for Risk Management Failure

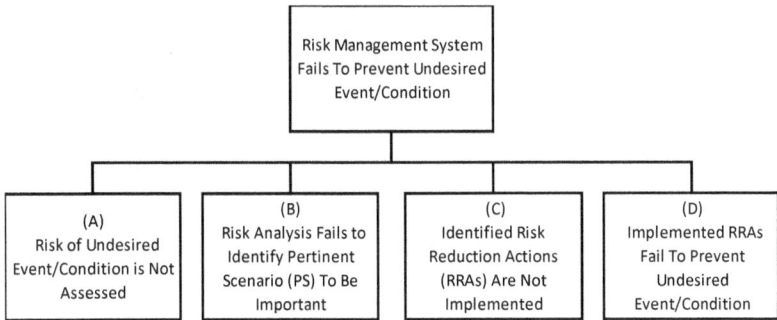

For a risk management failure to happen, at least one of the four conditions described in the second level must occur. The next exhibit then tracks how the four level 2 paths in the MLD line up with the questions from Part I and presents forward looking versions of the questions that can be used to examine proposed future activities.

Exhibit 10-2 Matrix of MLD Paths to Risk Management Questions

MLD Level 2 Path	Part I Backward Looking Question	Forward Looking Question
A) Risk of Undesired Event/Condition is Not Assessed	Was risk assessed for the scenario that actually occurred?	Was risk assessed for scenario that actually occurred?
B) Risk Analysis Fails to Identify Pertinent Scenario (PS) To Be Important	Did the risk analysis identify the pertinent scenario as important?	Did the risk analysis identify the pertinent scenario as important?
C) Identified Risk Reduction Actions (RRAs) Are Not Implemented	Were risk reduction actions taken to reduce likelihood and/or consequences?	Were risk reduction actions taken to reduce likelihood and/or consequences?
D) Implemented RRAs Fail To Prevent Undesired Event/Condition	Did implemented risk reduction actions work to prevent the event and/or mitigate the consequences?	Did implemented risk reduction actions work to prevent the event and/or mitigate the consequences?

In the balance of Part III we will shift our perspective on these four pathways from a backward examination of what went wrong with risk management in events that have already taken place to a forward looking view of how to spot weaknesses in risk management and make corrections before bad things happen. To begin this, I expanded the MLD presented above to include a third level as shown on Exhibit 10-3. In the chapters that follow, I will use this expanded MLD to help point out concerns that you should look for in considering how well risk is being managed in your world.

To continue the tie back to Part I, I also added a matrix at the bottom of the level 3 MLD that provides a more specific indication of the pathways to risk management failure taken by the three catastrophes from Part I. The "X's" in the cells of the matrix indicate my assessment of the relative importance of the path to risk management failure for each event. The more X's, the greater the importance. Note that multiple paths to failure were exercised for each event from Part I.

Exhibit 10-3 Level 3 MLD for Risk Management Failure

Risk Management System Fails To Prevent Undesired Event/Condition

(A) Risk of Undesired Event/Condition is Not Assessed
- A1: Pertinent Event/Condition Was Not Previously Known To Exist
- A2: Known Pertinent Event/Condition Was Deliberately Ignored

(B) Risk Analysis Fails to Identify Pertinent Scenario (PS) To Be Important
- B1: Risk Analysis Incomplete, Pertinent Scenario (PS) Was Not Identified
- B2: PS Identified But Consequences Are Underestimated
- B3: PS Identified But Frequency Is Underestimated

(C) Needed Risk Reduction Actions (RRAs) Are Not Implemented
- C1: No Effective RRAs Are Known to Exist
- C2: Clearly Identified RRA is Deliberately Ignored
- C3: Risk Was Knowingly Accepted. Additional RRAs Are Not Believed Necessary

(D) Implemented RRAs Fail To Prevent Undesired Event/Condition
- D1: RRAs To Avoid Risk Fail
- D2: RRAs To Transfer Risk Fail
- D3: RRAs To Control the Frequency of the PS Fail
- D4: RRAs To Control the Consequences of the PS Fail

	A1	A2	B1	B2	B3	C1	C2	C3	D1	D2	D3	D4
Macondo		XX	XX	X	X			XX				XXX
Great Recession		XX		XXX						XXX		
Fukushima		XXX		X	X			XX				XXX

106

Chapter 11 - EXCUSES FOR IGNORING RISK

> *There are known knowns. These are things we know that we know. There are known unknowns. That is to say, there are things that we know we don't know. But there are also unknown unknowns. There are things we don't know we don't know.*
>
> *Donald Rumsfeld*

Unknown Unknowns

In this chapter we will delve into path "A" from the risk management failure MLD. Path A1 from level 3 of the MLD tells us that risk management can be failed by a surprise scenario, something that has never happened before or, as stated famously by Donald Rumsfeld, things that we don't know that we don't know. Of course, this is true and this path is needed to make the MLD logically complete as we discussed in Chapter 7. But in my experience, real surprise events are not very common. Human experience is sufficiently robust that truly new events are quite special. Plus, the internet and other information technology advances have greatly enhanced our ability to access knowledge of past events, even very rare events. As evidence of this, let's look at a couple of examples.

First, in Chapter 3 we learned that the maximum probable earthquake estimated for use in designing the Fukushima plant was about 25% lower than the earthquake that actually occurred on March 11, 2011. So was this a surprise? From the internet, I was easily able to obtain a summary, in English, describing the very strong evidence that a great quake and tsunami had occurred in that same region of Japan in the year 869[11]. This information combined with the generally high seismicity of the area makes claiming "surprise" for this event very difficult.

---

[11] Jogan Sanriku earthquake, July 9, 869

Next let's consider the Islamic terrorist attack of 9/11/2001. Many seemed surprised by the use of airplanes as impact weapons, but this had been done before by the Japanese Kamikaze and Tom Clancy had used a rogue air liner against the U.S. Capital in *Debt of Honor* in 1994. So this threat certainly could have been foreseen.

The common thread in both these events and the thing to be on guard for with regard to surprise events is not so much the lack of knowledge but the failure to search for and actively imagine bad things. In no small part, it is the job of the risk analyst to think the unthinkable. The fact is that true surprises are so rare that I don't have a good example to give you. If anyone can provide me with a good example where competent risk management was defeated by a true surprise, please tell me about it!

The far more likely path to risk management failure through the A branch of the MLD is path A2, deliberate disregard of known hazards. Why would anyone do this, you might ask? In the balance of this Chapter I'll go over some of the reasons I've seen used by those that have taken this path to failure.

There's Too Much Uncertainty

Stop laughing! I know that this excuse might seem mind boggling but I can't count the number of times I've heard it used. How can uncertainty about the outcome of a proposed action be too large to assess yet the action itself prudent to undertake? I feel lucky?

Actually, this excuse needs a little deeper examination because there are some explainable reasons why it might be used that you can look for. First, this excuse could be used by someone who is truly immune to risk concerns or even actually seeking risk. I'll give you a tool to help recognize this type of behavior when I discuss risk management maturity a little later.

The more common reason for using this excuse comes from the discussion in Chapter 8 where I introduced the difference between probability and statistics. Some statisticians insist that the quantification of risk can only be performed using statistically significant data and that in the absence of robust data, no answer is possible. Thus, disciples of classical statistics will sometimes use excuse that "There isn't enough data" to assess risk. This leaves the conundrum of acting or not on a proposed question unanswered, but the ideology of classical statistics remains unblemished. Probabilists or Bayesians take a different view and use reasoned thinking to develop probability distributions to assess risk where "hard" data is not available. I am a card carrying member of camp #2 but acknowledge that this issue will not be resolved here.

I Can't Control That

Another excuse used to allow risk to be ignored is the lack of control over events. This excuse also comes in at least two forms. The first is a situation where the proposed action will be carried out in an environment that presents significant hazards that can potentially affect the outcome of an activity but those hazards are completely outside the control of the activity managers. A good example of this problem comes from large capital projects that take years to complete but will succeed or fail based on market conditions that will be known, with certainty, only after completion. This issue is a form of dependency, which I will address more completely in the next chapter, but for now let's just say that lack of control over what are often called external events does not mean that the risk from these events can be ignored.

The second flavor of this excuse is popular in governments or other large bureaucracies where responsibilities are compartmentalized to a degree where people begin to use the phrase "that's not my job". In such an environment people too often focus on the responsibilities they have been given and deliberately disregard anything else. To a degree, this attitude is understandable; everyone wants clear boundaries within in which they can act without being second guessed by others. And in turn, one must agree to stay out of other's business. But complex hierarchical organizations like this need some mechanism for aggregating the pieces of the enterprise into a whole. In recent years, this issue has been dubbed "enterprise risk management" (ERM) and a significant number of management consulting firms have warmed up to the business opportunity presented by this problem and put forward supposed solutions. Not surprisingly, these ERM solutions tend to look like whatever the management consulting firm was selling before it ever heard of risk management. If the firm specializes in information technology, then the enterprise risk management solution will be a big IT system. If the specialty was quality assurance, the solution will be a QA system, and so on. In other words, old wine in a new bottle. Although I will readily admit that I am not up to speed with all the approaches being used for ERM, I have yet to see any that really approach the issue from a risk perspective, rather than some other discipline being recast to address risk as an add on. You could say this finding is a corollary to the conclusion from Chapter 5 that genuine professional risk management help is hard to find.

So what is the right approach to use for enterprise risk management? I believe that there is no simple pat answer here. To be effective, enterprise risk management needs to be practiced at multiple organizational levels and different functional areas by many different people using methods and tools appropriate for each situation. In other words, risk management is really everybody's job and it needs to be practiced by people closest to a problem and most knowledgeable about it. But if risk management is practiced by frontline subject matter experts, how does integration get done? That is where the professional risk manager comes in. In any large and complex organization it is the professional risk manager who should insure that cognizant SME's have the skills and tools to be effective risk managers for their areas of expertise and that they are competently addressing the day to day risk issues relevant to their jobs. In addition, the professional risk manager should be responsible for creating and leading a higher level risk management system that can act to resolve risk issues that cross boundaries between operating organizations and look ahead to strategic risks that may emanate from external sources.

In other words, the key concept needed to make ERM work is the use of nested or layered risk management systems. On the first or bottom layer, risk management systems in frontline operating groups work continuously to identify and resolve problems that threaten performance objectives. If an issue cannot be resolved at the operating team level then it is passed up or promoted to a department level risk management system and in turn, if necessary to an executive level risk management system that is the final destination for difficult and strategic issues. The methods and tools used at each level must be effective and appropriate for each situation but in general, operating level systems will be data driven and work in something very close to real time. As you work up the risk management system ladder, the viewpoint will change to be increasingly forward looking and the risk analysis systems will increasingly rely on modeling and forecasting of future events rather than real time data.

I could say much more about ERM but I think it is time to get on to the next item in my list of excuses used for ignoring risk.

Cooked Books - Authoritarian Arrogance and Blind Ideology

I have struggled to come up with a really good title for this section that covers the most pervasive and destructive form of deliberate denial of risk, but whatever names I use to describe this type of behavior, it adds up to a pervasive bias in thinking that leads to destructive decision making. I'm not talking now about the rational exercise of value judgments in decision making that we will discuss in Chapter 13 but genuine prejudice. But because people can be skillful at rationalizing prejudice, this may not always be easy to recognize. Indeed it is easiest to see when it is most blatant. For example, when Iranian President Mahmoud Ahmadinejad makes statements like "there are no homosexuals in Iran" and "Israel must be wiped off the map", his insanity and dishonesty are on full display. But prejudice is more commonly rationalized through some form of "the ends justify the means" calculus that allows the practitioner to feel warranted in his or her actions, including active denial of the behavior. For example, it is not uncommon for project schedules and budgets to be arbitrarily set before bottom-up data driven schedules and budgets are developed. The rationalization for this behavior is that data derived goals always contain too much fat and that a project team needs to be challenged to meet aggressive goals. This is an example of authoritarian arrogance and, when practiced with moderation, might have some merit. But, I have also seen authoritarian arrogance carried to destructive levels and result in projects being initiated that were doomed to fail.

Another more pervasive rationalization for prejudice comes from religious or political ideology. This is on display almost every day in the actions of governments. The Iranian reference given above is an extreme example but it exists everywhere. In the United States, prejudice in justifying bureaucratic spending programs became so pervasive that in 1981 President Ronald Reagan issued an Executive Order requiring all significant new rules and regulations to pass benefit/cost analysis tests. Over the years some fabulous fictions have been created to comply with this order and they would be funny if they weren't so damaging. A classic example is the now infamous transfer of $716 billion in funding from Medicare to Obamacare that supposedly makes the later program affordable while not impacting the former at all.

Unfortunately, prejudicial sleight of hand maneuvers like the now-you-see-it-now-you-don't $716 billion are not always so easy to see.

Both of these destructive behaviors can be found in any environment but blind ideology is usually driven by extreme religious beliefs of partisan politics.

Spotting Prejudice at Work

So how can someone be expected to know if prejudice is being used to rationalize dangerous risk taking? Certainly, an active sense of skepticism toward hazardous endeavors is justified. But too many people allow healthy skepticism to morph into cynicism resulting in a prejudice against all new ideas. This can be as destructive to good risk management as the original sin of disregarding risk. In this and the next section I'll give you some ways to help tell the good dog from the bad dog before you get bit.

The first key to spotting bias is simply to do your homework. Major institutional decisions are always documented, often extensively. A prime example of this is the benefit/cost analysis requirement for U. S. government regulations that I mentioned earlier. But similar analyses, reports, cost estimates, schedules, and other supporting documents are very common and often available on the internet.

If you care about the outcome of one of these decisions, get the justifying analyses. Once you have the document, first check to be sure that the results actually support the actions being proposed. You may be thinking that any final decision must be supported by the underlying analysis but you must remember how powerful prejudice can be. Begin by looking for a rationalization that goes something like this: *the analysis of this decision indicates that an unwanted outcome is possible, but it didn't consider (insert excuses here) and so we are going to do what we wanted to do anyway.* Of course the actual conclusion won't be stated quite so straight forwardly so you may have to read it between the lines. When you find a decision based on a rationalization like this, run for the exit.

The second and more common method used to cover up prejudice is to cook the books or rig the results of the underlying analysis. Once you have been able to verify that the published results of an analysis does support the recommended decision, dig immediately into the analysis for the word *assumptions.* The assumptions are where you may be able to find

113

the tracks left by analysts that have been coerced into producing a desired result but wish to protect what remains of their integrity by documenting the torturous path followed to generate the cooked results. If assumptions are not clearly identified, you may have to hunt for them in footnotes, endnotes, or appendices. In Chapter 2, I documented some of the wildly indefensible assumptions made to justify the mortgage loan risks that led to the Great Recession.

If you cannot find the assumptions in some form, begin to worry and continue digging. If you can go on to identify analysis results and conclusions that are not thoroughly documented, then it is possible that the analysis is good but poorly documented, but it is also possible that the results were so biased that including the assumptions would have revealed their falsehood too easily. Poor documentation can be corrected by requesting further information, but if the documentation gaps cannot easily be closed, then you are probably looking at bias and it is now time to run for the exit.

One of the choicest examples of bias by assumption that I have ever seen was in a report from a well-known university dealing with global warming. If you are seriously concerned about carbon emissions, increased use of nuclear energy is a powerful, pun intended, strategy to reduce carbon emissions while continuing economic growth. But this university's prejudice against nuclear energy must have been even greater that their dislike for carbon emissions. To resolve this dilemma they concocted an assumption that using nuclear energy inevitably leads to global thermonuclear war and, therefore, nuclear energy cannot be included in any responsible energy strategy. Wow! What a whopper. The truth is exactly the opposite. Failure to use nuclear energy may leave billions of people without the economic capability to overcome poverty and build the stable responsible societies that reject war making. I wish I could document this wild example better, but the report that used it hit the bottom of my waste basket before I could think about saving it as a good example of blind prejudice by assumption.

Chapter 12 CAUSES OF RISK ASSESSMENT FAILURE

In this chapter we will examine path "B" from the risk management failure MLD. Path B failure represents any case where possible risks are acknowledged and an attempt is made to identify and assess their importance. The three possible sub-paths capable of producing risk assessment failure are identified in level three of the risk management failure MLD as scenario identification failure (Path B1), consequence underestimation (Path B2), and likelihood underestimation (Path B3). These three pathways align with the three fundamental risk assessment questions listed in Section 7 and the basic risk analysis steps outlined in Exhibit 7-1.

Scenario Identification Failure

Failure of a risk assessment to identify a scenario important to risk means that the scenario analysis process described in Chapter 7 was not performed comprehensively. Although Section 7 provides an introduction to the methods and tools that can be used to perform risk analysis, it is by no means a complete dissertation on the subject. Regardless of the particular methods and tools used, however, the robustness of any scenario analysis can be judged by examining it against the basic principles discussed in Chapter 7, including:

- Was the *system* under study well defined? Have all subjects important to risk been included or have important subjects been left out because they are too uncertain or somebody else's responsibility?
- Has the intended *success* of the planned actions been well defined with quantifiable metrics? Given that this question has been answered, has *failure* also been well defined with quantifiable metrics?
- Is the *physics* of the system well understood? Are limitations to our knowledge about what is being proposed acknowledged?
- Was a Master Logic Diagram (MLD) used to demonstrate completeness in the scenario analysis process?

Good answers to these questions should be easily found in any competent risk analysis, if they are not, worry.

Although failure paths B2 and B3 are separated to identify the underestimation of consequence and frequency, they have two common sources. The estimation of both involves two fundamental steps. First, basic event parameters are quantified based on the available knowledge about their occurrence. Then, these basic events are combined to produce a cumulative estimate of consequence or frequency. Thus, underestimation of consequence and/or frequency requires at least one of these two steps to be done incorrectly. Next we will discuss the leading reasons these errors are made.

Basic Event Underestimation

An introduction to the development of basic event data for both likelihood and consequence data was presented in Chapter 8. From Chapter 8, you should have come away with the understanding that the values of basic events are described by probability distributions. Sometimes, for convenience, we will use a point value to represent the whole distribution and, care needs to be taken when doing this to use only the mean value of the underlying distribution. OK, so what else can go wrong in the distribution development process? There are two significant issues that you need to be aware of here. One is widely recognized but still poorly understood, and the other is actually more important but seldom discussed. These issues are the proper use of Bayes Theorem and recognizing the difference between aleatory and epistemic uncertainty.

Bayes Theorem

I introduced Bayes Theorem in Chapter 8 and discussed its importance as the cornerstone principle of quantitative risk analysis. In a nutshell, Bayes Theorem defines for us the proper way to use available evidence to alter base beliefs and build representative probability distributions. Examples of the proper use of Bayes Theorem are plentiful in my earlier references and any text on probability. I will not repeat any of these examples here because in my experience real world problems will never manifest themselves in the carefully designed forms presented in the examples. Although conceptually simple, the proper application of Bayes Theorem requires skill and expertise that lies beyond this book. Even if you have pursued Bayes Theorem beyond my basic introduction and have gained a degree of familiarity with the mathematics, beware of using it for important decisions without review by an experienced analyst. Issues to be mindful of include the unfortunate reality that real world prior and posterior evidence never appears in the neat easily identified bins or categories that appear in common examples and that the proper weighting of evidence is challenging. The fundamental problem is that the human mind does not function intuitively to follow Bayes Theorem. Explanations for errors resulting from this problem are widespread and have been chronicled by many but the best source for a qualitative understanding that I have found is presented by Daniel Kahneman, who I referenced earlier. In *Thinking Fast and Slow* Kaheman describes, through the results of his research, how humans fail to properly employ Bayesian reasoning and how to guard against reasoning errors.

If you are feeling alarmed by all the red flags I have just waved in the above discussion, take heart. The fundamental problem Bayes Theorem tries to address is that people have a natural tendency to grab onto any piece of evidence that supports a pre-held belief and ignore other evidence that fails to support the base belief. Next, we will look at a somewhat more practical way of approaching this issue that you may find useful.

Aleatory and Epistemic Uncertainty

As important as Bayesian reasoning is to the development of basic event distributions, I have found in real world practice, an issue I think is just as important that you should be aware of in your efforts to manage risk.

Uncertainty can be divided into two components, *aleatory* and *epistemic*. Aleatory uncertainty is the inherent randomness that

117

remains after all relevant and available knowledge about an event or condition has been discovered. For example, for a fair coin, the aleatory uncertainty regarding the outcome of the next toss tells us that the probability of a head or tail is 0.5. Epistemic uncertainty, in contrast, is the uncertainty arising from imperfect knowledge about the event or condition in question. For the coin example, this would be questions about how fair the coin really is in producing heads and tails equally..

If we have some data that indicates the range of values that a parameter might occupy and we want to know how good this evidence might be for predicting future values, we can conduct a systematic review of the evidence to specifically focus on epistemic uncertainty. If we conclude from this review that our state of knowledge about this parameter is high/good, then we can infer that the uncertainty observed in the data is largely aleatory. If, however, the review indicates that our state of knowledge is low/poor, then the uncertainty observed in the future might come from unknown sources and fall outside the initially indicated range. Where the specific sources of epistemic uncertainty can be identified, it may be possible to initiate actions that improve our knowledge, reduce epistemic uncertainty, and improve predictability over what it would have been without the risk analysis. For the coin example, we might want to physically examine the coin and conduct some performance tests before allowing it to be used for anything important.

I call this state-of-knowledge type review a *Risk Factor Analysis* (RFA). The dye-in-the-wool Bayesians reading this will immediately jump to the conclusion that I am heading toward just a special application of Bayes Theorem (guilty, probably). But I have found the RFA approach for state-of-knowledge reviews to be useful and practical because you avoid the panic that can come just from using the term Bayes Theorem and, in a RFA, peoples pre-held biases can be approached indirectly making them easier to dislodge than if a direct confrontation approach is used.

So, what is an RFA and how is it done? The objective of the RFA is to systematically identify and evaluate potentially important risk conditions and events that will ultimately drive the top-level performance metrics for the activity and the overall program. The primary steps involved in conducting a risk factor analysis are:

➤ List activities, tasks or other elements that require examination.

➤ Identify applicable risk factors and develop a risk-ranking scale for each risk factor. A simple example is shown in Exhibit12-1.

➤ Rank risk for each activity for each risk factor and sum the results across each risk factor and for each activity per the simple example shown in Exhibit 12-2.

➤ Document the results and identify potential risk reduction actions for evaluation by the program team.

Risk Management Revisited

Exhibit 12-1 Example Risk Factors

RISK FACTOR	RISK CATEGORY		
	NONE/LOW (0/1)	MEDIUM (2)	HIGH (3)
Technology Maturity	Facilities & equipment involve only proven technology or new technology for a non-critical activity.	Facilities or equipment require the *adaptation* of new technology from other applications to critical construction or operating functions for this project.	Facilities & equipment require the *development* of new technology for critical construction or operating functions for this project.
Productivity Uncertainty	The planned rate of progress needed to reach completion as planned is conservative and well within benchmarks observed for similar tasks.	The planned rate of progress needed to reach completion as planned is aggressive but still within benchmarks observed for similar tasks.	The planned rate of progress needed to reach completion as planned is extremely aggressive or no benchmark experience is available to judge the reasonableness of the planned progress rate.
Equipment/ Material Cost Uncertainty	Equipment/ Material costs are well established and regulated by contracts or competitive market forces.	Equipment/ Material costs are not well established but should be regulated by competitive market forces.	Equipment/ Material costs are not well established and not subject to competitive market forces.

120

Exhibit 12-2 Example RFA Ranking Results

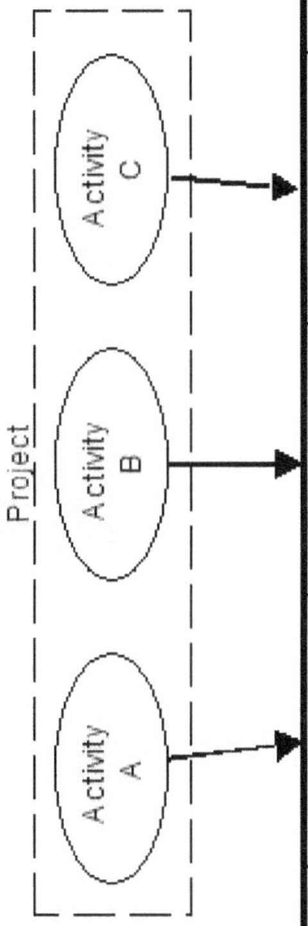

Risk Factor	A	B	C	Risk Factor Total
I)	Low (1)	Low (1)	High (3)	5
II)	Medium (2)	High (3)	Medium (2)	7
III)	Low (1)	Low (1)	High (3)	5
Activity Total	4	5	8	

Uses of Risk Factor Analysis Results

Simple qualitative RFA results like those shown in Exhibit 12-2 can be used in several ways to improve the risk analysis process. First, the qualitative risk factor rankings for each planned activity provide a first-order prioritization of risks before the application of risk-reduction actions. This general ranking process is shown by the activity total results given in the bottom row of the exhibit above. This example shows that, in order, activity C represents the highest risk, followed by B and then A.

The second use for RFA results is to identify possible risk-reduction actions responding to the identified risk factors. Risk-reduction recommendations are often straightforward to make from the RFA process and can be undertaken immediately without waiting for higher level risk results. When this is done, the RFA process can be updated and used to demonstrate early risk reduction progress. In addition, the systematic and comprehensive nature of the RFA process builds confidence in the program/project team as the RFA is performed.

The ultimate use for RFA results is, however, in the development of input distributions for quantitative risk modeling. As discussed in beginning of this section, RFA risk factors are intended to focus on epistemic uncertainty. That is because the RFA risk ranking questions are designed to reveal the strength or weakness in our state-of-knowledge about the activity in question. If all risk factor rankings can be reduced to "low" values, then the remaining uncertainty in a distribution predicting future performance for the activity in question should be primarily aleatory. But if significant epistemic uncertainty remains after the RFA is complete, then the resulting distribution predicting future performance for the activity should be correspondingly broader. Using this concept, the risk analyst and SME can work together to build guidelines for probability distribution development that are better representations of "truth" and more defendable than

122

distributions built by other means. An example of probability distribution development guidelines is shown below.

Exhibit 12-3 Example RFA Based Distribution Development Guidelines

Total Risk Factor Analysis Score	0 to 8, with no HIGH Risk Factors	9 to 12, with no HIGH Risk Factors	> 12 or HIGH Risk Factors Present
Overall Risk Rank	LOW	MEDIUM	HIGH
Adjustment Factor Guidelines	+/- 0% to 10%	+/- 10% to 20%	> 20% per specific assessment by the risk analyst
Generally Used Distributions	Triangular, Normal, Uniform, Discrete	Triangular, Normal, Uniform, Custom	Triangular, Lognormal, Custom
Confidence Level (Low/High) Assignment Guidelines	Low Value - 10% High Value - 90%	Low Value - 20% High Value - 80%	Per specific assessment by the risk analyst

Combinatorial Errors and Dependence

As interesting and important as basic event data development errors are in diagnosing risk analysis failures, they pale in comparison to the errors that can result when basic events are not combined properly. This subject was introduced in Chapter 8 where the right way to combine distributions was described along with the importance of using only mean values when combining point estimates. But the greatest errors in calculating scenario likelihood and consequence come from failures to recognize dependencies between events.

First some background. Two events are said to be statistically independent when the actual occurrence of either event has no effect on the likelihood of the other event also occurring. Coin tosses, with a fair coin, are the classic example of independent events. When knowledge of the outcome of an event does change our assessment of the likelihood of the second event, these events are said to be dependent. The dependency can be strong, meaning that knowledge of one event gives us perfect knowledge of the other outcome or, the dependency can be weak with knowledge of one outcome only giving us partial knowledge of the second event. By far, failure to recognize and account for dependencies is the greatest contributor to Path B failures in the risk management failure MLD.

We have observed the dependency problem already in the Part I events. Major contributors to the Great Recession were assumptions made that mortgages in all regions of the U. S. could not go bad at the same time and that credit default swaps could provide protection because the underlying securities could not all go bad at the same time. Wrong! In the safety realm, errors of many orders of magnitude can occur if unrecognized dependencies exist between events that are of low likelihood and presumed independent. These types of dependencies are called *common cause failure mechanisms* and they often dominate risk analysis results for highly redundant systems. The four reactor melt downs at Fukushima resulted from the common cause failure of many cooling and containment systems following the earthquake and tsunami.

The academic aspects of dependence are far beyond the scope of this book and can be researched on-line and in any academic text on probability and statistics. What I want to do here is take a very practical look at how dependencies can be identified and accounted for in a risk analysis so that you can know what to look for in a well done analysis and, contrarily, what to worry about if you can't see a comprehensive treatment of dependencies.

First, let's talk more about the complexity of this issue. In the introduction above I described dependence as an issue between two events, but remember that in Chapter 7 I described a risk analysis as being composed of many scenarios. Scenarios are in turn composed of many events and for any event in the scenario, dependence can exist with any of the preceding events. Plus, other dependencies can occur between any combination of events in the scenario. Thus, the mathematical

124

possibilities for the existence of unique dependencies can be mind boggling. Don't despair, but this is one reason why risk management needs to be done by a recognized professional.

Identifying Dependencies

Remember that back in Chapter 7, I described one of the essential steps in performing a risk analysis was to understand the physics of the system under study. Perhaps the greatest challenge within this task is the search for dependencies. This is kind of like looking under rocks for snakes; you hope not to find anything, but the penalty for not looking and being surprised later is too great to ignore. Let's get your mind started on this subject by describing some of the types of dependencies that can be found in the universe.

Functional

Functional dependencies are the type of hardwired or engineered connections that need to be understood and accounted for to perform a credible risk analysis for any system. In physical systems, they involve the connections between and among structures, systems, and components. In a power plant, for example, all pumps driven by electric motors depend on the electric power system. Or, a heat exchanger may depend on water flowing from the component cooling water system. Functional dependencies also exist in electrical, data processing, and any type of defined system. A tool that can be used to identify and document functional dependencies is the dependency matrix that systematically charts the dependence, if any, of one system element against all others. An example is shown in Exhibit 12-4.

Exhibit 12-4 Example Dependency Matrix

		FT FAST DB TRANSFER		DC ESSENTIAL DC		EP ESSENTIAL AC		SW SERVICE WATER		SC SAFEGUARDS CHILLED WATER		CW COMP COOLING WATER	
		A	B	A	B	A	B	A	B	A	B	A	B
FT FAST DB TRANSFER	A	▨				[1]		[5]		[5]		[5]	
	B		▨				[1]						
DC ESSENTIAL DC	A			▨		[1]		[2]		x		x [3]	
	B				▨		[1]		[2]		x		x
EP ESSENTIAL AC	A					▨		[4]		x		x	
	B						▨		[4]		x		x
SW SERVICE WATER	A					[2]		▨		x		x	
	B						[2]		▨		x		x
SC SAFEGUARDS CHILLED WATER	A	[7]				[6]				▨			
	B		[7]				[6]				▨		
CW COMP COOLING WATER	A											▨	
	B												▨

NOTES:

[1] IF DC_x FAILS, AC_x SUCCESS REQUIRES SUCCESS OF FT_x, X = A OR B

[2] IF BOTH SW_x AND FT_x FAIL, THEN AC_x FAILS, X = A OR B

[3] MAY BE ABLE TO KEEP NORMALLY RUNNING TRAIN RUNNING

[4] AFFECTS 1 SW PUMP, BUT OTHER PUMP IN TRAIN MAY STILL WORK

[5] LOAD SHED WILL TURN OFF NORMALLY RUNNING PUMP IF ON SAME SIDE AS A FT FAILURE

[6] PROLONGED LOSS OF CHILLED WATER MAY CAUSE FAILURE OF SWITCHGEAR

[7] BLACKOUT CAPABILITY INSURES 2 HOURS OF DC WITHOUT OVERHEATING BATTERIES

Human Action

In risk analysis, human actions are specific actions required by humans in the context of a risk scenario. These are things that people are trained and drilled to perform by rote procedure. There are two types of human action errors. Failing to perform a required action promptly and correctly when needed is an error of omission. Performing a damaging action outside of procedural guidance is an act of commission. Human action errors have been key contributors to many catastrophes including the Three Mile Island nuclear accident and many airplane crashes. The modeling of human actions in a risk analysis is a subject I have not discussed before and one that is generally beyond the scope of this book. I introduce it now because it is a form of functional dependence that can be critically important in systems that require human actions for success. The issue of dependence is especially important in analyzing human actions because experience has shown that once a human makes one error, the likelihood of subsequent errors rises dramatically.

Spatial

As the name implies, spatial dependencies are those caused by the particular location of things to each other. Going back to the power plant again, all the equipment in a room will be affected by a fire in that room, even if they have no other relationship to each other. In other systems, these spatial dependencies can be harder to identify. For example, in 1989 a very serious airplane accident[12] occurred when a jet engine broke apart in flight and shrapnel from the engine cut all otherwise "independent" hydraulic lines to the flight control surfaces. There are no shortcuts to understanding spatial dependencies. Only the comprehensive mapping of spatial relationships can reveal these issues. Thankfully, computerized three dimensional design programs make analyzing spatial dependencies much more manageable for new systems, but many older systems designed and built before the computer era may contain undiscovered spatial dependencies.

Bayesian knowledge based
This dependency exists where a poor state of knowledge about an event or condition is recognized and plans to update weak data with new information can be performed. For example, let's say I want to estimate the cost and schedule performance for a project that consists of some number of special tasks for which I have poor knowledge from experience. To address this problem I could mock up or simulate the task in some way to gain experimental data or I could wait until the first representative task is actually completed in the project and then employ Bayes Theorem to update the estimates for the remaining tasks. The failure to actively monitor real data and promptly update performance estimates has been fatal to many projects.

Beyond project risk, Bayesian or knowledge based dependencies exist whenever the acquisition of new knowledge would materially change the assessed risk for an activity.

---

[12] United Airlines flight 232, July 19, 1989.

External or Systemic

External dependencies can be overlaid on any of the types of dependencies already discussed, but they are distinguished by their ability to impact all tasks or events within an activity simultaneously. An earthquake, for example, shakes an entire facility all at once. In another example, the profitability of millions of otherwise independent financial transactions could be impacted by a single change in the tax code.

Voodoo

This final category of dependency is reserved for relationships between seemingly unrelated events that unambiguously exhibit non-random behavior. In other words, there seems to be a connection but we are not able to identify any causal mechanism, hence Voodoo. Attempting to list examples of Voodoo dependencies here would probably offend some so I'll pass and hopefully avoid having any spells sent in my direction.

On a serious note, be very careful when considering the use of dependencies where causation is not definitive. For example, after the very devastating hurricane season of 2005, climate change advocates were quick to claim that in the future storms would be more frequent and more severe. However, it is now 2014 and no hurricanes have hit Florida (my home) the past eight years.

Modeling Dependencies

Knowing now that we need to look for dependencies and what types of things to look for, how can you tell if a risk model has done a good job of identifying and assessing dependencies?

Fault trees, introduced in Chapter 7, are a modeling tool specifically conceived to document and quantify functional dependencies in engineered systems. The simple example presented in Chapter 7 is but the tiny, tiny tip of the iceberg. Actual fault trees for complex systems can be enormous and require specialized software to be manageable, but they are an essential tool. If they have been employed in a risk analysis, it should be quite evident. Event trees also can be used to model functional as well as other types of dependencies. To do this the risk analyst must specify the dependency by changing the values used for split fractions based on the conditional outcome of prior top events. This can be done directly by the analyst for small models, as you will see in Part IV. Or, for large models, by writing split fraction logic rules that automatically change split fraction values based on the instructions given. This also requires specialized software tools. Influence diagrams are another modeling tool that can be used to identify and assess dependencies. As the name implies, influence diagrams are often used to examine non-engineered systems where the dependencies may be weak and only "influence" the outcome of other events.

As indicated earlier, the modeling of human actions in a risk analysis is generally beyond the scope of this book. In any activity requiring human actions for success, however, they are probably an essential contributor to risk. If the activity you care about includes important human actions, be especially alert to this subject and only accept a human actions risk analysis that includes possible dependencies between actions.

For spatial dependencies, there are no shortcuts. The positions of key structures and components relative to each other and the available pathways between them must be documented and assessed. Prior to three dimensional computer design programs this was an arduous task and was often done with severe assumptions. For example, any fire in a room could be assumed to fail all equipment in the room, no matter how small the fire or how big the room. With 3-D design software spatial dependencies can be identified and assessed much more comprehensively.

State of knowledge type dependencies tend to be harder to recognize than they are to assess. As discussed in Chapter 12, admitting our lack of knowledge, or ignorance, is sometimes difficult and requires a deft approach like Risk Factor Analysis to reveal these. Once identified though, state of knowledge dependencies can be assessed with several techniques that broadly fall under the category of "what if?" or sensitivity analysis. Sensitivity is an extremely valuable tool and should be part of all risk assessment results. Some state of knowledge dependencies need an even more direct approach to produce the most useful results though. One good example of this comes from project risk analysis. In a project there are two fundamental types of activities. The first is task based and the duration and cost will be determined by task specific scope and technical factors such as unit rates and the cost of material. The second activity type also has task specific input factors but its duration is determined by the time needed for other activities. These are called umbrella or accordion activities because they need to expand to cover whatever duration is needed. Project management is a typical example. To correctly assess project risk the umbrella activities must be modeled as a function of overall schedule duration. Not getting this state of knowledge dependency right is a mistake that any good risk analysis should catch.

When I discussed the use of assumptions back in Chapter 11, I portrayed them in a negative light because I was pointing out their possible use as a cover for analysis results that can't pass the ho-ho test. But even in the most comprehensive and objective analyses, assumptions play an important role in defining the external limits or boundaries of the effort. Documenting these limits or boundaries is important because even the best analysis can be appear faulty if its results are misused outside of the valid application area defined by the authors. To help prevent this from happening, I prefer to construct a boundary conditions event tree to define the scope and important limits of the analysis. In the Exhibit 12-5 example, the feasibility of a project was evaluated and a recommendation made to proceed. However, two key assumptions regarding the scope were made that, if forgotten, could alter the feasibility decision. So, to make these assumptions abundantly clear, the example boundary conditions event tree was constructed and placed prominently in the assessment rather than buried in analysis notes.

130

Exhibit 12-5 Example Boundary Conditions Event Tree

Project Boundary Conditions	#18 Site Included in Project?	Number of Sensors Converted?	#	Scenario Description
	yes	3,600	1	Project Baseline
		11,500	2	Significant additional costs & cutover time needed for 8,000 added sensors
	no	3,600	3	Small reduction in cost possible from reduced communications system scope.
		11,500	4	Savings from deliton of #18 is dwarfed by costs for added sensors

Statistical correlations are the final tool I will discuss for modeling dependencies and the reason is because I recommend their use as a last resort. Correlations are a powerful tool and are widely described in academic texts. They are also straightforward to specify in modern Monte Carlo analysis software tools. So why am I listing them last on the tool list? First, as a practical matter, they can seriously increase the run time needed for a risk model, if widely used. The more serious issue, though, is the effect they can have on the results of the analysis. Correlations have the effect of locking uncertainty in place through the Monte Carlo process. If this is in fact true and the correlation is an important part of the risk analysis story being told, fine. But the analyst should recognize what is happening inside the simulation and explain why you should have confidence in the observed result.

One final caution needs to be issued before we leave the subject of dependencies. Thus far I have emphasized the importance of not missing dependencies, in other words, making the error of assuming independence when dependencies lurk below ready to bite. But there is another edge to this sword that can also cut you. With modern analysis tools it can be easy to model risk issues at extremely fine detail. Generally, modeling more detail is considered good because greater fidelity will provide more precise understanding of a subject. But there is a trap you need to watch for. When pressing the fidelity of a model to ever greater levels of detail, consider the degree to which true independence between the model elements can be defended. If similar activities have been divided for modeling just to increase the apparent level of detail, then intrinsic correlations can exist between the elements. If independence is then assumed in the quantification process, the results will then contain too little uncertainty. This error stems from the *central limit theorem* which states that the distribution for a sum of independent random variables tends to be normal in form and that the variance of the distribution of the sum decreases as the number of random variables increases. If you need some clarity for the fog I just laid down, please consult any probability text or online article on the subject for more detail. But the bottom line is this. If intrinsic dependencies are present, then the central limit theorem is not valid and a Monte Carlo simulation assuming independent distributions can give a misleading result.

Project risk management again provides a prime example of the intrinsic correlation problem. Widely used critical path management software easily allows the modeling of project activities in great detail. And there are legitimate project management reasons for doing this. When evaluating project risk, however, the independence of the activities may be hard to defend at the lowest levels of the work breakdown structure. For example, a project may contain a thousand piping installation tasks at the lowest level of the work breakdown structure. The risk factors that will determine the level of uncertainty in executing these tasks may, however, affect all one thousand tasks. If risk calculations are performed at the thousand tasks level of detail with the activities assumed to be independent, the results will show much less uncertainty in schedule duration and cost than actually exists. To avoid this error, risk needs to be assessed a higher level of the project work breakdown structure.

Finally, use of any or all of the methods described above are good indicators that the issue of dependence has been considered in a risk analysis but, because of its importance, you should also find a specific discussion of how dependencies were addressed in any comprehensive risk assessment.

Chapter 13 - FUMBLING THE RISK MANAGEMENT BALL

In this chapter we will examine paths "C" and "D" from the risk management failure MLD. Path C failure represents cases where the important contributors to risk have been identified by a risk assessment and risk reduction actions (RRA's) identified to mitigate the important contributors but risk management failure is experienced because the proposed risk reduction actions were not implemented.

Three possible sub-paths capable of producing risk assessment failure are identified in level three of the risk management failure MLD. In Path C1, no RRA's are taken because none are known. This path is of course possible and needed to make the MLD complete. However, in my experience, there are always mitigating actions that are possible. In the extreme, the assessed risk associated with a proposed plan of action can always be avoided by not initiating the proposed action.

MLD paths C2 and C3 both involve the acceptance of risk associated with a proposed plan of actions. In path C3, planned actions are initiated after the rational application of needed risk reduction actions have been made and residual risks judged to be acceptable. In MLD path C2, proposed actions are taken without a rational assessment of benefits and costs or initiated in spite of an assessment that rejects the proposed actions. It's time now to talk a little more about what "rational" decision making is. In Chapter 9, I discussed the basics of how to use benefit/cost analysis and risk goals to determine the acceptability of a proposed action. In that discussion I presumed that the decision maker would accept the objective evidence presented by the risk analysis and act rationally based upon that evidence. In the real world, however, we know this is not always the case. MLD failure path C2 specifically calls out the case where clearly identified risk reduction actions are deliberately ignored. This causes an unnecessary exposure to risk that can be avoided if the identified RRA's are implemented. Why would anyone do this?

133

It is not my intent here to go into a dissertation on utility theory and decision making so I'll try to keep my comments simple and practical. The reasons why people behave irrationally are of course the subject of many books and papers that I will not attempt to explain, even if I could. What I can do is alert you to this issue and point out some signs of irrational behavior in action. From the perspective of risk management, it is possible for an individual or an organization to be irrational in several ways. To describe different categories of risk management behavior, I have prepared what I call the risk management maturity matrix shown in the next exhibit. The first category in the matrix is *risk prone* behavior that is described by path C2 of the risk management failure MLD. This is the acceptance of unnecessary, avoidable risk. The second type of risk irrationality is *risk ignorant* that, as the name implies, describes behavior that simply ignores risk. The next category is *risk compliant* which is a condition prevalent in government bureaucracies and regulated industries. Perhaps the most perverse category is *risk averse* behavior. This is the rejection of expected benefits that unambiguously exceed manageable risks for a proposed activity. This type of irrationality is not directly addressed in the MLD because it does not lead to risk management failure for a specific activity since the proposed activity is not attempted. At a higher level of risk assessment, however, risk aversion is a serious strategic flaw that can cause an individual, organization, or nation to perform sub-optimally. The final category describes the *risk proactive* behavior that we should all try to achieve.

Exhibit 13-1 Risk Management Maturity Matrix

		Risk Management Maturity Level			
Characteristics of Behavior		Risk Prone	Risk Ignorant	Risk Compliant	Risk Averse	Risk Proactive
Risk taking posture	Actively disregards obvious hazards	Acts without considering hazards	Acts after obvious hazards addressed as required by regulation	Exaggerates frequency & consequences of hazards, seeks deminimus risk	Acts with confidence when assessed benefits >> risks
Use of objective data gathering and analysis	None	Anecdotal and incomplete	Used minimally as required by regulation (punching the ticket)	Comprehensive, but emphasis is placed on not repeating past failures	Comprehensive, objective and timely
Use of testing and prototyping	None	None	Used minimally as required by regulation (punching the ticket)	Over done, past the point of diminishing returns	Used prudently to improve knowledge of benefits and risks
Attitude toward regulation	Actively ignored	Passively ignored	Regulations viewed as excessive, minimal compliance is assumed to insure safety	Regulations viewed as minimal requirements, over compliance is assumed to be necessary to insure safety	Regulations viewed as necessary but not sufficient, compliance is not assumed to insure safety
Use of qualitative risk ranking	Used perversely to justify high risk actions	Used anecdotally	Used minimally as required by regulation (punching the ticket)	Used widely with conservatively skewed results	Limited use as screening tools & input to QRA
Use of quantitative risk analysis, modeling & simulation	None	None	Used minimally as required by regulation (punching the ticket)	Limited use with conservatively skewed results	Comprehensive & objective with uncertainty assessed for both benefits and risks

Path D failure represents cases where the important contributors to risk have been identified by a risk assessment and risk reduction actions identified and implemented. For these cases, however, risk management failure is still experienced because the risk reduction actions fail to provide the needed protection.

Four possible sub-paths capable of producing risk reduction action failure are identified in level three of the risk management failure MLD. These four sub-paths correspond to the four categories of risk reduction actions discussed in Chapter 9.

In order to fully understand path D, we now need to discuss what success and failure really mean. Risk management success does not mean that we never experience failure or realize a loss. Going back to Part I, please pause for a moment and answer the following questions.

1. If the blowout preventer had successfully sealed the well and prevented a blowout after the rig explosion and fire, would the Macondo event be viewed as a risk management failure?

2. If banks had been able withstand the 2007-8 downturn in housing prices without requiring government bailout, would the event be viewed as a risk management failure?

3. If the Fukushima emergency generators had been able to provide emergency cooling water to the reactors and prevent core melt after the Tōhoku earthquake & tsunami, even though the plants would never be able to generate power again, would the event be viewed as a risk management failure?

Remember to always evaluate risk management performance against the top event in the master logic diagram. As you will see in the Part IV example risk analysis, it is typical for a risk analysis to define several different end states that describe partial failure or degraded performance as well as complete success and total failure. Obviously we would prefer to experience complete success in every endeavor, but this is not realistic. Partial failure end states offer the opportunity to better understand risk and make analysis results more useful, but should not be used as the benchmark for defining risk management success.

OK, but in our Part I examples risk reduction actions did fail to prevent catastrophe and I indicated this in Exhibit 10-3. So how does this happen? First, remember that other pathways to risk management failure were also indicated in Exhibit 10-3. But path D failure can happen and it is a serious when it does. The most common cause relates back to MLD path B and dependencies. Recall my discussion of dependencies. There I said that the greatest errors in calculating scenario likelihood and consequence come from failures to recognize dependencies between events. I actually copied that sentence so I would repeat it exactly because it is worth remembering. Unrecognized dependencies turn out to also be the predominant reason for MLD path D failure as well. To press the point home, let's review the role of unrecognized dependencies in our Part I catastrophes.

In the Macondo event, I concluded that the drilling team thought that the blowout preventer was bullet proof and this led them to accept risks with drill string integrity that they might not have otherwise. Unrecognized was the need for the drill string to be properly aligned with the blowout preventer.

Leading up to the Great Recession still faceless manipulators created boundary conditions governing mortgage creation and securitization that deliberately covered up dependencies between financial instruments, institutions, and markets. This allowed reckless lending and financial engineering to go on for years prior to market collapse under the pretense of good practices.

Beyond deliberately lying about the seismic hazard that existed at the Fukushima site, Japanese engineers failed to recognize and/or failed to act to break the dependence of multiple cooling pumps on electric switchgear that was vulnerable to flooding.

Unfortunately, sad stories like these are not that rare. In response, a philosophy for managing risk in high consequence conditions has been developed to address this problem. The central tenant of *Defense in Depth* is to create multiple independent and redundant layers of defense to compensate for potential multiple failures so that no single layer of protection, no matter how robust, is exclusively relied upon. When considering the possibility of MLD path D failure, always look to see if defense in depth has been employed.

Chapter 14 - THE RISK MANAGEMENT REVIEW

In the introduction to Part III, I stated that its objective would be to create a forward looking view of how to spot weaknesses in risk management and make corrections before bad things happen. To complete this task I have condensed the key issues that have been discussed in Part III into a checklist that I hope many will find useful for performing a risk management review. The desired or preferred answer to each question is indicated in the GOOD column.

Exhibit 14-1 Risk Management Review Checklist, Page 1

Question	Reference	Review Score Good	Review Score Not Sure	Review Score Bad	Comments
Risk Management Comprehensiveness					
Was the system under study well defined?	Chapter 7	Yes			
Has the intended success of the planned actions been well defined with quantifiable metrics?	Chapter 7	Yes			
Has failure also been well defined with quantifiable metrics?	Chapter 7	Yes			
Is the physics of the system well understood and have limitations of knowledge been acknowledged?	Chapter 7	Yes			
Have important risk issues been left out because they are too uncertain or somebody else's responsibility?	Chapter 11	No			
Have analysis assumptions been used to ignore risk?	Chapter 11	No			
Is there any indication that performance goals or objectives were influenced by authoritarian arrogance or political ideology?	Chapter 11	No			
Risk Analysis Completeness and Accuracy					
Have both inductive and deductive tools been used to demonstrate completeness in the scenario analysis process?	Chapter 7	Yes			
Has a Risk Factor Analysis (RFA) or other method been used to identify epistemic risk?	Chapter 12 Exhibits 12-1 & 12-2	Yes			
If point estimate calculations were performed, were only mean values used?	Chapter 8 Exhibit 8-6	Yes			

Exhibit 14-2 Risk Management Review Checklist, Page 2

Question	Reference	Review Score			Comments
		Good	Not Sure	Bad	
Does the risk analysis present a comprehensive description of the treatment of dependencies?	Chapter 12	Yes			
Are functional dependencies clearly identified?	Chapter 12 Exhibit 12-4	Yes			
If human action dependencies are important, are they clearly identified?	Chapter 12	Yes			
If spatial dependencies are important, are they clearly identified?	Chapter 12	Yes			
Are knowledge based dependencies clearly identified?	Chapter 12	Yes			
Are external or systemic dependencies clearly identified?	Chapter 12 Exhibit 12-5	Yes			
Are statistical correlations used in the quantitative risk analysis?	Chapter 12	Yes			
Has the possible presence of intrinsic correlations been considered in the risk quantification?	Chapter 12	Yes			
Effectiveness of Risk Reduction Actions					
Would you characterize the risk management maturity of the subject organization as *risk proactive*?	Exhibit 13-1	Yes			
Has a risk informed approach been used to identify and implement risk reduction actions (RRAs)?	Chapter 9 Exhibit 9-9	Yes			
Was a defense in depth strategy used to insure RRA effectiveness?	Chapter 13	Yes			

Part IV – Risk; Through a Glass Darkly

> *What we see now is like a dim image in a mirror; then we shall see face to face. What I know now is only partial; then it will be complete, as complete as God's knowledge of me.*
>
> *1 Corinthians 13:12*

Chapter 15 - DEFINING BAD

Now that we have completed a whirlwind journey through the world of risk management and looked at how it should be done and how it sometimes gets off track, let's see if we can apply what I've covered to do something useful, or at least interesting. In Part I, we reviewed some really bad events and examined how risk management failed in each case to prevent the event. But tragic as these events were, they are nowhere near as bad as we can imagine. Fiction, and especially science fiction, provides us with a never ending array of apocalyptic events and dystopian visions. As of this writing, *Divergent* is the current rage.

But there is also a very serious side to the consideration of catastrophes. As an engineer who worked at Los Alamos National Laboratory, I know better than most how devastating it would be to ever have even one of our weapons actually used. At the same time, I believe that the assured destruction that would come from the use of nuclear weapons has prevented Earth's major nation states from making war with each other for the last 69 years. This, combined with the economic and political globalization policies adopted by the United States and its allies since World War II, has resulted in an era of peace and prosperity unprecedented in the history of human civilization[13].

---

[13] This is not just my opinion, see MFRA references 55 & 60.

So what could spoil the party? As I mentioned in the first paragraph, our writers and film makers are constantly coming up with inventive visions of our demise. These range from the downright silly disaster flicks (I think *Sharknado* pegs the needle here) to very plausible pictures of possible futures that are not bright at all. But what if we use the risk assessment methods and tools we have talked about in this book and take a cold blooded objective look at what could happen to turn our hard won civilization on end. How would an objective assessment of possible catastrophes line up with Hollywood version? Let's see.

To begin, we'll go back to the essential steps for performing a risk assessment listed in Chapter 7.

Define the system –
We will examine possible risks that could disrupt the continued welfare and even the continued existence of human civilization.

Define Success and Failure –
A rich set of possible metrics exists that could be used to measure the success or failure of human civilization. Metrics for the more qualitative aspects of civilization like political freedom, religious freedom, or economic opportunity would be interesting but difficult to define. Economic output, environmental, or health metrics like life expectancy would easier to define but not totally relevant to big picture questions. So that still leaves us with human fatalities as the metric of choice. Just to be clear, we will look at what risk analysts call prompt fatalities, which are fatalities that unambiguously result directly and promptly from a defined risk scenario.

Per the U.S. Census Bureau, the current human population of the Earth is about 7.2 billion. Extinction scenarios, by definition, would need to cause sufficient fatalities to prevent survival of the species. That would be pretty close to a 100% fatalities scenario. One percent survival would leave nearly 72 million people, a pretty viable population. But I don't think we need to have a total extinction event to get our attention. The most catastrophic event we look at in Part I was the Tōhoku earthquake & tsunami which killed about 20 thousand people. This event certainly got the attention of the world, but the loss of life amounted to about .00028% of the world's population, hardly a threat to the survival of the species.

So what would be an appropriate level on the human fatalities scale to use as a benchmark for our inquiry? In 2012, about 56 million people died worldwide from all causes[14]. This is about 154,000 every day. The vast majority of these deaths result from normal causes of aging and disease. Per World Health Organization data, about 9% of the total or about 5 million people per year die from all types of injuries and accidents, including warfare. These deaths would fit our definition of prompt fatalities and would average something less than 13,000 per day worldwide. Now let's look beyond the averages to see how big individual mass casualty events have been. The worst large scale prompt fatality events experienced in recent history are listed below.

Exhibit 15-1 Recent Events with High Human Fatalities

Estimated Fatalities	Cause	Location	Date
92,000	Mount Tambora volcano	Indonesia	4/10/1815
140,000	Nuclear Weapon	Hiroshima, Japan	8/6/1945
230,000	Earthquake and Tsunami	Indian Ocean	12/26/2004
316,000	Haiti earthquake	Haiti	1/12/2010
500,000	Bhola cyclone	Bangladesh	11/13/1970
650,000	Tangshan earthquake	China	7/1/1976
1,000,000	Floods	China	7/1/1931
1,000,000	Hong Kong flu	worldwide	1968–1969
2,000,000	Asian flu	worldwide	1957–1958
75,000,000	1918 flu pandemic	worldwide	1918–1920

I compiled this list from unverified sources found on the internet and make no claim that it is completely accurate or comprehensive. These are all prompt fatalities from short duration events except for the epidemics that are considered one event even though they occurred over several years. If

---

[14] 2012 World Population Data Sheet, Population Reference Bureau

accumulated over their total duration, total deaths from wars would present even larger numbers.

A conclusion I think we can make from the above data is that there is a long distance on the prompt fatalities scale between the events that we as a species have experienced so far and any Armageddon type scenario. From a risk management perspective, this tells us that if we were to assess only doomsday risks, we may miss some really important things that lie between what we have seen so far and the end of days. Accordingly, I suggest that we define the scenario consequences that we will search for to be *one million or more prompt fatalities within ninety days of the scenario's initiating event*. I also think that an appropriate name for this exercise would be a *mega-fatality risk assessment* or MFRA.

Understand the Physics -
To guide us through what can go wrong in the risk management process, I have made extensive use of the master logic diagram first presented in Exhibit 10-1, so I hope you are now comfortable with this tool. Using the consequence level described above as the top event, I have constructed the MLD shown below to guide the MFRA.

Exhibit 15-2 Master Logic Diagram for Mega-Fatality Risk

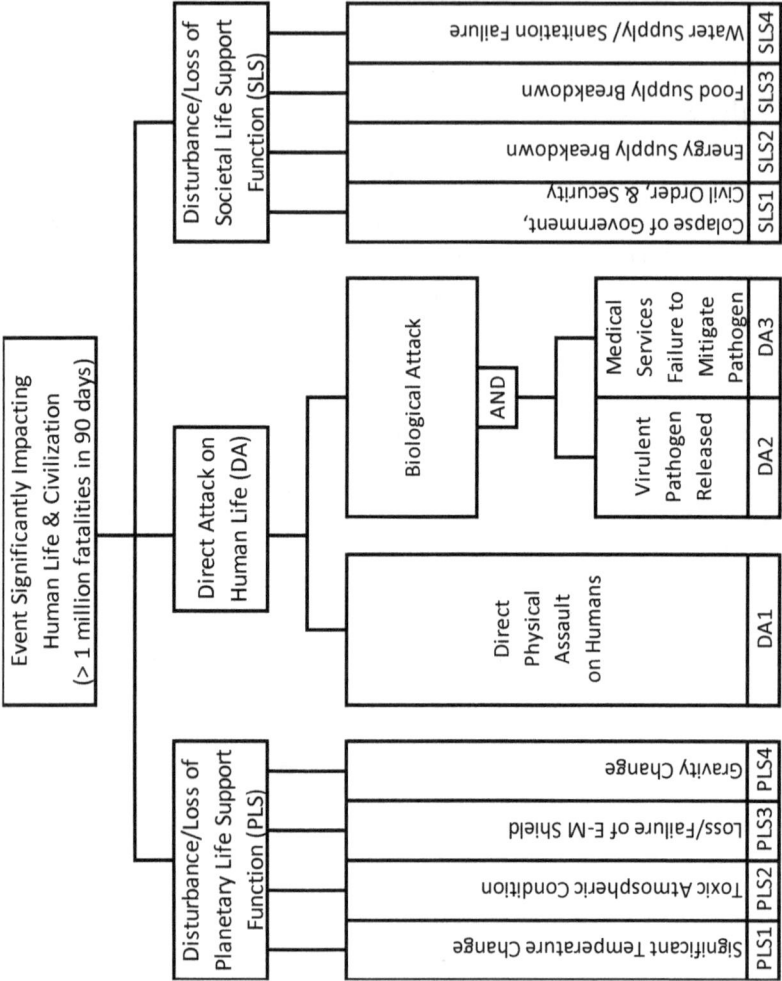

Remember that a MLD is used to demonstrate logical completeness in the risk assessment process. In this case, if the logic shown in the MFRA MLD encompasses all the pathways that could produce the top event, then the risk assessment is logically complete. Remember too that the MLD does not quantify the risk. To do that, we will need to construct a list of scenarios that, when matrixed against the MLD, trigger at least one pathway through the MLD to the top event. The process of constructing the scenario list also helps verify the MLD logic. An example of how this is done was provided earlier in Exhibit 7-17.

Before building the MFRA scenario list, let's talk a bit about the MLD logic and some interesting features it presents. The MLD logic says that a large number of people can be killed by direct attack (DA path) or by interrupting one of the systems needed to support human life. These life support systems operate on the planetary level (PLS path) providing us with environment we live in and at the societal level (SLS path) providing the safety, food, water, and energy we all need. The DA and PLS paths probably come as no surprise to most readers. The SLS path may be less obvious.

Throughout most of human history, people generally lived in subsistence mode. That is they spent most of their time and energy seeking the basic necessities of life and, they found or failed to find those things in close proximity to where they lived. As civilization evolved, people gathered together and individuals began to specialize according to their abilities in ways that improved the collective welfare. But for thousands of years specialization largely remained local and the provision of basic human needs remained very simple. This began to change meaningfully with the emergence of modern technologies following the Renaissance. Technology advances simultaneously reduced early mortality and enabled agricultural and industrial production to expand rapidly. By early in the nineteenth century, the global population had reached one billion, and at the outbreak of World War II it was just over 2 billion. During the conflagration of this war, the degree to which people had become dependent on specialized societal support systems was made apparent by the deaths of as many as 25 million people from starvation and disease not related to military actions.

But since WWII, the era of peace, prosperity, and accelerating technology I described earlier has allowed the world's population to more than triple. Today's systems that provide us with food, water, energy and other essential services today have become almost incomprehensibly complex. Hundreds of millions now live with little knowledge of how the food, water, and energy they consume is produced. If these societal life support systems should suffer any kind of prolonged interruption, the loss of life could be enormous. This is the reasoning I used to include the SLS path in the MFRA MLD.

The level 3 SLS pathways in the MFRA MLD probably deserve discussion as well. The SLS1 pathway encompasses the governmental functions that provide physical safety and security. Intra-national violence or civil war (strange name) would fall in this path.

Energy supply systems (SLS2) are complex and interdependent but the focus here should first and foremost be on electric energy. Except for small amounts stored in batteries, electric energy must be created continuously as it is needed, and boy, is it needed. Almost every activity in modern life requires electric power in some way. Food can't be gathered or processed without electrical equipment. Water and sewer pumps don't work without it. Gasoline pumps at the filling station won't work either. Oh and computers, phones, and televisions, not for very long. Some critical facilities, like hospitals, have emergency generators but these will only run for a day or so until their fuel supplies are gone. Many people would be quick to add air conditioners and elevators to the critical list too, as soon as they try living without these things for a while.

Electric energy is also a critical focus for risk assessment because of it fragility. We are all familiar with short duration and small scale electric system interruptions caused by bad weather or equipment malfunctions. But electric power systems are also susceptible to large scale, long duration outages as well. The prolonged loss of electric power caused by the Tōhoku earthquake was a contributing factor to the Fukushima Daiichi reactor meltdowns. But large scale electric power outages could also be caused intentionally. On April 16, 2013 gunmen disabled one of the largest electric substations in California in 19 minutes[15]. According to the same reports, an unpublished federal government analysis indicates that a coast to coast electric outage could be caused by the simultaneous disruption of as few as nine such substations. In addition, it has long been known that the electric grid can be disabled by an electro-magnetic pulse (EMP) generated by the detonation of a nuclear weapon at high altitude. At least one natural act of God, solar storms, is also a threat to electric power systems. MFRA references 11 through 25 provide quite thorough discussions of these issues.

Our food supply system (SLS3) is vulnerable in at least two ways, interruption and contamination. For short term effect, contamination is by far the easier of the two. With mass communication systems in full operation, it takes only a very small amount of contamination to start a panic response that can, at least for a while, compromise the entire system. Small contamination acts will, however, not kill many or last very long. Large scale, sustained contamination would, in contrast, be much harder than interruption because of the large amount of contaminant material needed and the large organization needed to carry it out. Significant interruption of the food supply though is possible by leveraging any of the system's many dependencies such electric power, fertilizer, or fuel for machinery.

Similar to food supply, the water and sanitation system (SLS4) is vulnerable to both interruption and contamination. The same comments made above also apply here but even more so.

---

[15] Wall Street Journal, 2/5/14

Water supplies are more independent than food supplies. A contaminated food item could cause a panic anywhere the item can travel to. Water contamination though is only a local event unless it is a derivative of an atmospheric contamination event.

Many readers may also wonder why a fifth path is not included in the SLS pathway to include the breakdown of medical services as a critical life support system. This is a good question. The reason is that in normal, non-emergency time, only a small percentage of people would genuinely require medical services for survival within a 90 day period as defined by our top event. The availability of or lack of medical services will certainly make an important difference in the outcome of many catastrophic events, but singly, the unavailability of medical services for 90 days will not cause the top event to occur. Note that in the case of a pandemic, the failure of medical services (DA3) is required to produce the top event. DA3 failure could result from a technical inability to control a pathogen or because medical services were specifically targeted for destruction as a prerequisite to a biological attack.

Chapter 16 - LISTING BAD

The next step in the MFRA risk analysis process is to identify conceivable events that, if they occur, could propagate through at least one pathway of our MLD to the top event. As we saw in Chapter 7, matrixing these scenarios against the MLD basic events helps organize the quantification process and verify the logical completeness of the MLD. We will now proceed to build this list of conceivable scenarios and then return in the next chapter to the quantification task.

We will start by examining the high fatality events from Exhibit 15-1 that have actually occurred. Although I did not claim this table to be a complete list of high fatality events, I will claim that it is complete enough to conclude that there are insufficient actual events to allow a comprehensive list to be compiled by historical review using classical statistics. Thus, to build the list we will have to use imagination and subjective reasoning. Buckle up.

To build the initial list, I first decided to categorize events based on whether they occurred naturally or were caused by human actions. I further divided the natural category into cosmic events for those originating beyond the planet Earth and terrestrial events for those occurring planet side. Human events were subdivided into aggression by nation states, terrorism, and other event and accidents. I separated terrorism from "normal" warfare because we as a civilized species have developed behavioral norms and conflict resolution mechanisms that are at least somewhat effective in regulating the behavior of nation states in their relations with each other. Although persons and disaffected groups with terrorist ambitions have always been with us, the fragility of complex modern civilization and the power of advanced technologies have given terrorists the potential capacity to disrupt normal life in unprecedented ways on enormous scale. Our collective capacity for dealing with terrorism and particularly the aftermath of a successful terrorist attack is relatively less well defined. As a result, I felt terrorism deserved special attention for MFRA risk assessment.

To populate the list I began with the types of events that have already occurred as listed in Exhibit 15-1 and added obvious candidates such as various forms of warfare and extreme consequences from known phenomena. Next I surveyed the internet and literature sources for conceivable doomsday scenarios. Informative sources I found included the following:

- B John Garrick, *Quantifying and Controlling Catastrophic Risks*, Academic Press, 2008, IBSN 0123746019.

- Nick Bostrom and Milan M. Cirkovic *Global Catastrophic Risks*, Oxford University Press, 2008. IBSN 978-0-19-857050-9

- Existential Risks - Threats to Humanity's Future. http://www.existential-risk.org/

- Martin Rees, *Our Final Hour* (2003), Basic Books, IBSN 0-465-06862-6

- The Global Catastrophic Risk Institute (GCRI). http://gcrinstitute.org/

- The Future of Humanity Institute. http://www.fhi.ox.ac.uk/

- The Future of Life Institute (FLI). http://thefutureoflife.org/

I also found several articles in *Wikipedia* to be very useful.

Next I turned to the world of fiction for ideas. Apocalyptic visions are endemic in our culture and date back at least to the Book of Revelation. The first work in modern literature to deal with the end of man is believed to be Mary Shelley's 1826 novel *The Last Man,* which is a story about a group of people as they struggle to survive in a plague infected world. Cataloging all the books and films that have been made since then that present some vision of the apocalypse would require another book or more. Still, fiction does serve as a legitimate source for ideas. Sorry *Sharknado* fans, you didn't make the cut.

It's just about time to look at the events list but before giving the list a careful review, let me add some clarifying comments. First, note that the events listed in the tables are really just example scenarios. In the next chapter we will add some questions and caveats to help clarify the scenario definitions and aid quantification. This may increase the number of scenarios. For example, an initiator might only become a mega-fatality event under worst case conditions. We will try to take this into account. Next, be aware that the list does not include long term gradual decay type events like climate change, regression to barbarism, or descent into religious totalitarianism. This is because we have defined our top event to focus on prompt fatalities over a short period. If mankind succumbs to any type of long term decay scenario, it will probably contain multiple mega-fatality events of the type we are studying here. Thus, long term trends might have an influence on the likelihood of specific events, but mega-fatality events can still happen with, or without, the long term trend. Also, note that the example scenarios are listed in these tables as if they were independent events. This is not necessarily true. For example, biological attacks and nuclear attacks are listed separately in the tables. However, the consequences of a biological attack might be vastly increased if medical services for the targeted population were deliberately destroyed prior to release of the pathogen. We will address these issues and more in the next chapter.

With that, the events identified for inclusion in the MFRA risk analysis are listed in the following exhibits.

Exhibit 16-1 Natural Events Selected for MFRA

EVENT DESCRIPTION	PLS1	PLS2	PLS3	PLS4	DA1	DA2	DA3	SLS1	SLS2	SLS3	SLS4
Cosmic Events											
Random asteroid/comet strike on Earth	X				X					X	
Solar electromagnetic storm					X				X		
Supernova storm					X			X	X		
Alien attack on Earth	X	X		X	X	X		X	X	X	X
Alien contamination toxic to human life						X	X				
Universe ends, God terminates the existence of our universe	X	X	X	X	X	X	X	X	X	X	X
Natural Terrestrial Events											
Super volcanic eruption with ash ejection that cools the planet	X										
Great earthquake and/or tsunami strikes a highly populated area					X						
Exceptionally severe cyclone/hurricane strikes highly populated area					X						
Other extreme flood event strikes highly populated area					X						
Extreme drought and famine										X	
Other food crop failure and famine										X	
Magnetic pole reversal			X								
Pandemic results from a naturally occurring disease						X	X				

Exhibit 16-2 Human Initiated Events Selected for MFRA

EVENT DESCRIPTION	MLD BASIC EVENTS										
	PLS1	PLS2	PLS3	PLS4	DA1	DA2	DA3	SLS1	SLS2	SLS3	SLS4
Military Conflict											
Civil war					X			X			
War between nations with conventional weapons					X			X			
War between nations with chemical weapons					X						
War between nations with biological weapons							X	X	X	X	X
War between nations with nuclear EMP weapons								X		X	X
War between nations with nuclear attacks on human populations	X				X		X	X	X	X	X
Acts of Terrorism											
Political assassination escalates to war (WWI)								X			
Mass murder attack and possible military retaliation					X			X			
Electric power system sabotage and possible military retaliation									X		
Biological laboratory sabotage and possible military retaliation						X	X		X	X	X
Nuclear terrorist attack and possible military retaliation					X			X			
Biological weapon attack and possible military retaliation						X	X	X	X	X	X
Other Human Initiated Events & Accidents											
Accidental release of known disease		X				X					
Accidental release of engineered pathogen		X	X			X	X				
Accidental detonation of one nuclear weapon					X						
Accidental creation of new toxic/hostile life form			X			X	X				
Accidental creation of a toxic environmental condition		X	X	X							
Government collapse & revolution leads to military conflict								X			
International financial/economic crisis leads to government collapse & military conflict								X	X	X	
Breakdown of societal life support functions								X	X	X	X

Chapter 17 - QUANTIFYING BAD

To quantify mega-fatality risk we will build a risk model using event trees as described in Part II. This requires the identification of initiating events, event tree questions and split fractions that define the possible scenarios that may evolve from the initiator, and end states for each scenario that describe the possible consequences. Probability distributions will be used to describe our state of knowledge about each initiating event, split fraction, and end state. The distributions will be combined using a Monte Carlo simulation program.

After following me this far through the risk management story, I hope your reaction now is *no sweat, let's do this!* Here we go.

If my opening paragraph left you with any questions about how the quantification process will work, I have prepared the graphic below that describes the overall architecture of the MFRA risk model.

Exhibit 17-1 MFRA Risk Model Architecture

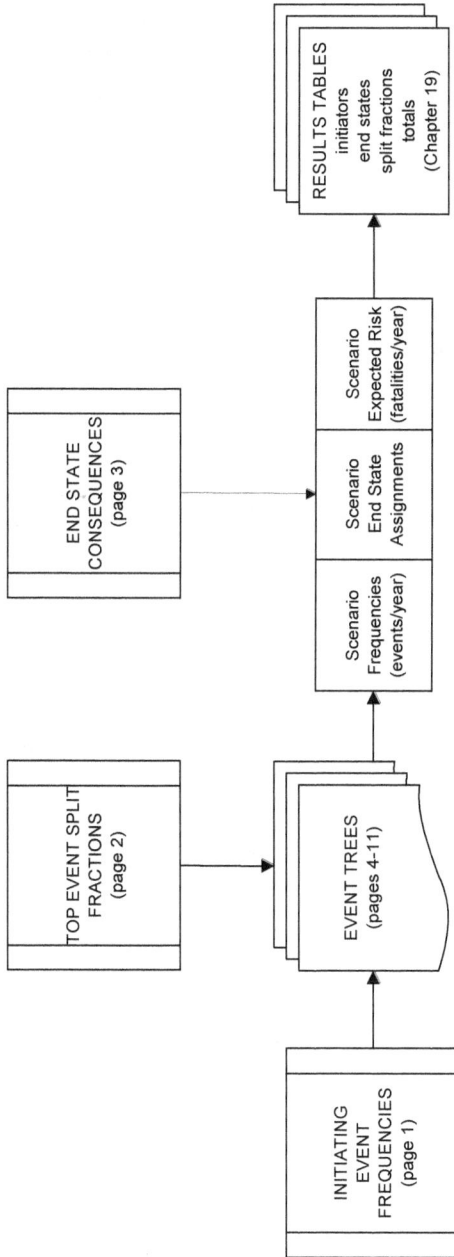

All of the components of the risk model depicted in the exhibit are presented in Chapter 20 except for the results which are presented first in Chapter 19. The software used to construct and calculate risk model results is *Microsoft Excel* with an add-in Monte Carlo simulation tool from Oracle Corporation called *Crystal Ball*. *Crystal Ball* allows the values in the spreadsheet cells to be probability distributions instead of point values. It will also combine distributions using the Monte Carlo method and place the resulting distribution in a designated cell. Cells containing distributions are highlighted in the spreadsheet pages shown in Chapter 20. I have not included listings of the actual equations used or probability distribution details since these require familiarity with the software to understand.

In the balance of this Chapter I will discuss, for each initiating event, the development of the initiating event frequencies, the construction of event trees, the development of split fraction conditional probabilities and the calculation of scenario frequencies. All these elements of the MFRA risk model can be found in Chapter 20. For the most part I will not repeat the numeric values from the risk model in the text, so you might want make copies of some of the key data tables to facilitate following along as you read. In the next chapter I will describe the definition of scenario end states by consequence category and the development of probability distributions for prompt fatality consequences. Finally, in Chapter 19, I will summarize and review the results of the MFRA.

Scenario Likelihood Analysis

As discussed in the previous chapter, the events listed in Chapter 16 are only example scenarios or categories of scenarios. In order to build a risk assessment model, decisions must be made about how to represent these events in an event tree format for quantification. These decisions are based on risk modeling experience and are driven by many factors including the availability of evidence for building distributions and the facilitation of meaningful results. In other words, it is important that the risk analysis not only gives a concise result, but also it must reveal the important contributors controlling the final result. Notes about why I built the MFRA event tree model the way I did are summarized in the following exhibit and discussed in the balance of this chapter.

Exhibit 17-2 Modeling Notes for Natural Events

EVENT DESCRIPTION	MODELING NOTES
Cosmic Events	
Random asteroid/comet strike on Earth	4 initiating events defined to represent strikes from different size objects. Also, the frequency for a 10km strike (1E+8) forms a credible cutoff for other existential events
Solar electromagnetic storm	One initiating event created for worst case storms
Supernova Storm	No supernova candidate stars are believed to be close enough to Earth to threaten us.
Alien attack on Earth	Not quantified, no basis exists to establish a frequency > 1E-8.
Alien contamination toxic to human life	Not quantified, no basis exists to establish a frequency > 1E-8.
Universe ends, God terminates the existence of our universe	Not quantified, no basis exists to establish a frequency > 1E-8.
Natural Terrestrial Events	
Super volcanic eruption with ash ejection that cools the planet	2 initiating events defined for the largest possible categories of eruption
Great earthquake and/or tsunami strikes a highly populated area	One initiating event created for worst case quakes
Exceptionally severe cyclone/hurricane strikes highly populated area	One initiating event created for worst case floods
Other extreme flood event strikes highly populated area	One initiating event created for worst case storms
Extreme drought and famine	Despite predictions of calamity, food production has kept pace with population growth. The food supply system is, however, very complex and fragile. Any disruption of the food supply system can quickly lead to famine at least on a local or regional scale. Thus, famine is modeled primarily as a secondary consequence of initiators that disrupt societal life support systems.
Other food crop failure and famine	Despite predictions of calamity, food production has kept pace with population growth. The food supply system is, however, very complex and fragile. Any disruption of the food supply system can quickly lead to famine at least on a local or regional scale. Thus, famine is modeled primarily as a secondary consequence of initiators that disrupt societal life support systems.
Magnetic pole reversal	Many pole reversals have occurred during the time of life on Earth, no evidence exists of catastrophic effects (Ref. 10).
Pandemic results from a naturally occurring disease	One initiating event created to evaluate a spectrum of possible pandemic severity levels.

Exhibit 17-3 Modeling Notes for Human Initiated Events

EVENT DESCRIPTION	MODELING NOTES
Military Conflict	
Civil war	Modeled as an end state resulting from multiple scenarios.
War between nations with conventional weapons	Modeled as an end state resulting from multiple scenarios.
War between nations with chemical weapons	Modeled as an end state resulting from multiple scenarios.
War between nations with biological weapons	Modeled as an end state resulting from multiple scenarios.
War between nations with nuclear EMP weapons	Modeled as an end state resulting from multiple scenarios.
War between nations with nuclear attacks on human populations	Modeled as an end state resulting from multiple scenarios.
Acts of Terrorism	
Political assassination escalates to war (WWI)	Modeled as an initiator that can result in war.
Mass murder attack and possible military retaliation	Modeled as an initiator that can result in war.
Electric power system sabotage and possible military retaliation	Modeled as an initiator that can result in mega fatalities and broader war.
Biological laboratory sabotage and possible military retaliation	Modeled as an initiator that can result in mega fatalities and broader war.
Nuclear terrorist attack and possible military retaliation	Modeled as an initiator that can result in mega fatalities and broader war.
Biological weapon attack and possible military retaliation	Modeled as an initiator that can result in mega fatalities and broader war.
Other Human Initiated Events & Accidents	
Accidental release of known disease	Modeled as an initiating event
Accidental release of engineered pathogen	Not quantified, but the pathogen in all biowar scenarios is assumed to be of high severity.
Accidental detonation of one nuclear weapon	Not quantified, nuclear weapons are not normally located in high population areas. Thus, accidental detonation should not cause a mega fatality event.
Accidental creation of new toxic/hostile life form	Not quantified, no basis exists to establish a frequency > 1E-8.
Accidental creation of a toxic environmental condition	Not quantified, no basis exists to establish a frequency > 1E-8.
Government collapse & revolution leads to military conflict	These events can lead to civil war which is included in armed conflict.
International financial/economic crisis leads to government collapse & military conflict	Modeled as an initiating event
Breakdown of societal life support functions	Modeled as a consequence of other initiators.

161

Cosmic Events

Random asteroid/comet strike on Earth (KI10m, KI100M, KI1km,KI10km)

We begin our discussion of the MFRA model with kinetic impact events. I found that both the frequency and direct impacts of potential kinetic impact events to have been comprehensively researched (references 1, 2, and 3). I elected to model kinetic impacts by defining four categories of events based on object size with frequencies as listed in the initiating event table in Chapter 20.

First, for smaller size objects with a nominal diameter of 10 meters (KI10m), significant fatalities should only be produced if the object impacts near a high population area. To estimate this likelihood, I added a top event question in the KI10m event tree to ask for the conditional probability of a kinetic impact near a high population zone. The split fraction for the conditional probability of a high population zone impact (HPZ) was estimated by assuming that a 10 meter object must strike within 50 miles of a high population area to produce significant prompt fatalities. With an estimated 550 target cities with populations greater than one million on the Earth, I calculated the conditional probability of a high population zone hit (HPZ) at about 2%.

For a strike by medium size objects with nominal diameters of 100 meters (KI100m) and 1 kilometer (KI1km), direct blast and impact effects will be observed on a local (KI100m) or regional (KI1km) scale. Estimation of the resulting direct prompt fatalities is discussed in the next chapter. Indirect effects from the failure of societal life support systems (SLS) would also be possible and will be discussed later.

Impact by a large kinetic object with a nominal diameter of 10 kilometers (KI10km) will produce significant direct blast and impact effects that will be experienced globally. Debris from the impact ejected into the upper atmosphere is expected to produce significant global cooling for an extended period impacting multiple food crop cycles. This should guarantee the failure of societal life support systems and result in a near or complete extinction of higher life forms, including humans. This is estimated to occur at a mean frequency of 1E-8 per year.

Screening of low frequency events
The KI10km event also provides an important benchmark for structuring the balance of the MFRA risk analysis. Since the KI10km event yields human extinction at a mean frequency of 1E-8, we can use this frequency to screen other lower frequency events and focus the MFRA on events of higher likelihood. The screening process is illustrated by the simplified risk curve shown in the exhibit below. KI10km effectively produces a frequency floor for the risk curve. Events with frequencies less than 1E-8, no matter how severe, cannot significantly contribute to the risk results because of the floor created by KI10km. Thus we can focus the balance of the analysis effort on events that will shape the risk curve above KI10km as indicated.

Exhibit 17-4 Screening of Low Frequency Events

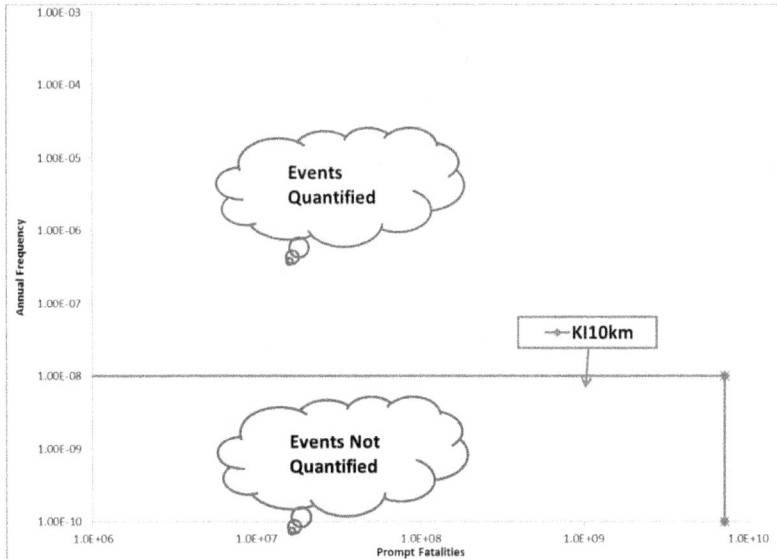

The events eliminated from further consideration by this process are indicated in the modeling notes tables and listed below.

- Supernova Storm
- Alien attack on Earth
- Alien contamination toxic to human life
- Universe ends, God terminates the existence of our universe
- Accidental creation of new toxic/hostile life form
- Accidental creation of a toxic environmental condition

Solar electromagnetic storm (SolStrm)

In addition to the normal energy output that makes the Earth habitable, the sun routinely fires out extra bursts of energy that can be harmful if they strike Earth. These bursts of energy or solar storms consist of three major components: solar flares, solar proton events (SPEs) and coronal mass ejections (CMEs). Not all solar storms produce all three elements but the largest solar storms do. The most severe solar storm recorded in recent history occurred on August 28 through September 2, 1859. This is called the Carrington Event named after British astronomer Richard Carrington who actually witnessed the instigating solar flare. Electromagnetic energy from this solar storm electrified telegraph lines, shocking technicians and setting their telegraph papers on fire. Other observed impacts included the Northern Lights spreading as far south as Cuba and Hawaii and auroras over the Rocky Mountains so bright that they woke campers because they thought it was morning. (Ref #11). Because of our increased reliance on electric and electronic systems, a similar solar storm today would have a much more severe impact on society that it did in 1859. A prolonged loss of electric power and societal life support systems dependent on electric power would be experienced over at least the region of Earth most directly impacted by the solar storm. A further discussion of consequences for this and other loss of electric power events will be included in the next chapter.

The initiating event frequency estimated for a solar storm of Carrington Event severity is based on data from references 11, 12, and 13.

Natural Terrestrial Events

Super volcanic eruption (SuperV7 & SuperV8)

Volcanic eruptions occur often and can be quite spectacular but they seldom cause significant human deaths because the ground motion, lava, and ash flows are generally local in nature and not near high population zones. It is possible, however, for an eruption to be so violent that the mass ejected reaches the upper atmosphere and disperses to blot out the sunlight. The resulting cooling could last for an extended period impacting multiple food crop cycles. If severe enough, regional and global failure of societal life support systems could occur and result in significant human fatalities.

To gauge this risk, a volcanic explosivity index (VEI) has been defined to measure the severity of eruptions. The VEI contains nine levels designated zero through 8. Ejecta from VE-1 through 6 eruptions is capable of producing short term effects such as air travel disruption but only VEI-7 & 8 are potentially severe enough to cause lasting regional or global cooling. The only eruption in this severity range to occur in modern times was the VEI-7 eruption of Mount Tambora in Indonesia in 1815. Global cooling was experienced through 1816 and is known as the year without summer. Frequencies for these events were estimated using data from reference 4. Top events were also included in the event trees for SuperV7 and SuperV8 to assess the severity of societal life support systems failure that might result from these events.

Great earthquake and/or tsunami (Mquake)

As illustrated by the data I presented in Chapter 3, large earthquakes are actually quite common with quakes of magnitude 8 or 9 occurring at a rate of almost one per year, per USGS data (reference 6). Per the USGS data, no earthquake/tsunami has yet killed enough people to meet the one million prompt fatalities threshold for the MFRA. But with human populations steadily increasing, especially in areas where little investment is made in seismic risk reduction, I think it is only a matter of time until this unfortunate threshold is met.

For the MFRA model, the USGS historical data on M8 and M9 earthquakes was used to establish the initiating event frequency, and then I included a top event to ask if the quake occurred near a high population area, similar to KI10m.

Exceptionally severe cyclone/hurricane or other flood (Mflood)
I chose to aggregate all types of flooding events, other than tsunamis, together under this initiator for the MFRA risk model. Reference 7 indicates that the only historical flood events to meet our fatalities criteria have been river floods. It may be that the seemingly more severe cyclones/hurricanes present less risk because people typically have advanced warning of their arrival allowing time for evacuation while river floods caused by a dam or levy break can strike with little warning. In any case, the initiating event frequency is based on data from reference 7 and since the historical events did meet our one million fatalities criteria, impact on a high population zone is guaranteed at this frequency.

Extreme drought or other food crop failure and famine
Despite many warnings, food production in modern times has been fully able to keep pace with an increasing human population. A review of the historical data for famine events indicates that the most severe famines have been consequences of other events such as war and ideological persecution. These other events brought about what I characterize in the MFRA risk model as a breakdown of societal life support systems. As a result, I chose to account for famine in the MFRA risk model as a consequence of other events rather than an independent initiating event.

Pandemic (NatEpid)
Pathogens capable of causing great harm to humans are a constant threat. A significant fraction of all humanity is employed in health care services and the battle to prevent and treat disease never ends. Over time amazing progress has been made by medical science in this war, but it remains far from won. Antibiotic resistant strains of old diseases and species hopping bugs present new threats. As of this writing the world wide health care system is scrambling to contain an Ebola outbreak in western Africa.

Representing pandemic risk in the MFRA model presents a significant challenge. The threat a pathogen presents to humans is determined by a complex set of factors that include characteristics of the pathogen itself, how it infects humans, how humans can be protected from infection, how long it incubates before symptoms appear, how it can be detected, how it can be treated after detection, and of course, how lethal it is to humans. Faced with this complexity, I elected to use a rather simple data based approach for modeling pandemics rather than attempt to build a physics based model.

I began by developing an initiating event frequency based on recent experience from all types of epidemics (reference 26). I then parsed this frequency into three levels of severity with split fractions also based on actual recent experience. For each severity level I then questioned the likelihood that medical services would be able to successfully contain the outbreak and prevent a mega fatality scenario. The failure probabilities assigned to these split fractions ((CFL, CFM, and CFH) may seem counterintuitive because I estimated the lowest failure rate for the most severe events. This is because "take two aspirin and go to bed" may be an effective response for low severity infections, but the medical services community is prepared to use much more aggressive methods for more severe outbreaks (reference 27). Finally, for medium and high severity outbreaks that are not contained by medical services, I included a top event question to ask if other societal life support systems would be affected by the pandemic. This can happen when the disease or just fear of the disease causes people to abandon their normal work and shelter at home.

The development of end states for each of the resulting pandemic scenarios is discussed in the next chapter.

War

While discussing the development of the initial events list back in Chapter 16, I indicated that I thought "normal" warfare should be separated from terrorism for our evaluation. This is because we are collectively less well prepared to address terrorist acts as a source of potential conflict than we are the old fashioned territorial and other types of disputes that have caused past wars. As a result, terrorism might be more likely to cause future wars than the past initiators. But when attempting to develop the logic to incorporate this idea into the MFRA, I came to the conclusion that both the old and the new sources of conflict could end up at the same place. To handle this and still be able to distinguish between the various possible initiators, I elected to define general categories of warfare as end states and then build event trees that would allow different scenarios with different initiators to take separate paths to these common warfare end states. The architecture for the approach is illustrated in the following exhibit.

Exhibit 17-5 Architecture for War Scenarios

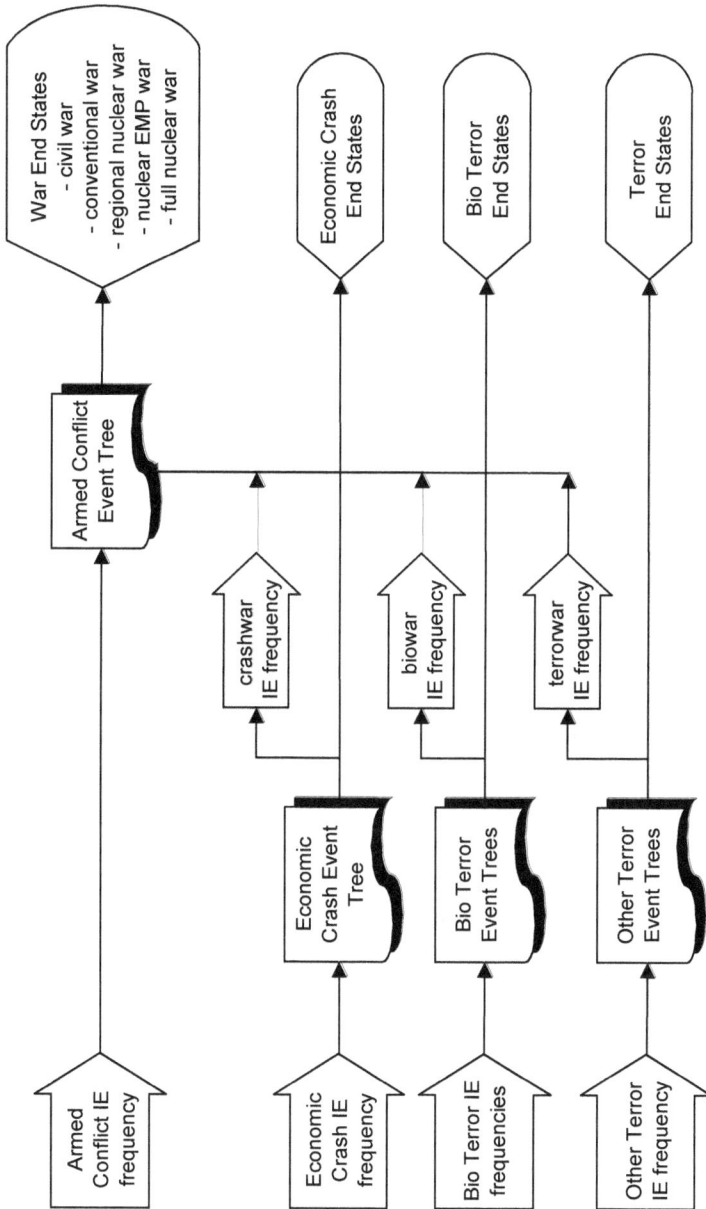

Allow me to make some clarifying comments about the architecture shown above.

- The armed conflict initiating event frequency (armcon) is based on data from references 53 & 54 for wars that occurred between World War II and the terrorist attack on 9/11/2001. I felt this period would provide the most representative data for future conflicts not caused by terrorism.

- The armcon event tree structure contains five top events that parse the initiator into nine end states representing different types and severities of possible wars. Note that all nine are not all listed in the exhibit.

- Scenarios from event trees for other initiators can produce frequencies for both direct consequences and retaliatory military strikes. These retaliatory strike frequencies (terrorwar, biowar and crashwar) are then used as initiating events and directed through the armcon event tree structure using appropriate split fractions for each initiator to calculate the frequency of war end states caused by terrorist attacks or other non-traditional sources of conflict. In total, war end states can be reached from nine different initiating events.

- Frequencies from all scenarios leading to each specific war end state can then be summed to determine the total for each war end state.

Armed Conflict (armcon)

The armcon event tree contains the following five top event questions.

1. Scope of conflict?

This question parses the initiating event frequency into three possible paths. They are civil war, regional conflict, and global scale conflict. This last category designates conflicts that involve significant coalitions of nations including at least one nuclear weapons state and a significant intensity of fighting. The split fractions (RWAR and GWAR) were estimated using data from references 53 and 54. Three conflicts were designated as global scale; the Korean War, the Vietnam War, and the Gulf War.

2. No nuclear EMP weapons used?
This question asks if the conflict escalates to the level where nuclear electromagnetic pulse (EMP) weapons are used. Since EMP weapons would not directly injure people, it is possible that a combatant might rationalize that EMP weapons could be used without invoking a full scale nuclear response. I assumed that EMP weapons would not be used during a civil or regional war because at such short range, their effects would be felt by the attacker. The split fraction (EMPAC) value of (0.01) is my estimate.

3. No other nuclear weapons used?
This question asks if the conflict escalates to the level where nuclear weapons are used against human targets. I made no distinction between tactical (small) and strategic (big) nuclear weapons. The split fraction NWGW is defined as the likelihood of escalation to nuclear weapon use from conventional war by a nuclear arms state in a global conflict and was assigned a base rate of 0.01. This base rate was decreased .005 for escalation to nuclear weapon use in a regional conflict (split fraction NWRW). The likelihood of escalation to nuclear use against human targets was increased to 0.5 following the use of EMP weapons (split fraction NWEMP).

4. SLS systems maintained?
This top event question asks if societal life support systems (SLS) are maintained during a conflict. Later in the assessment of consequences, the prompt fatalities resulting directly from military conflict will be increased for scenarios where SLS systems also fail. SLS failure is assumed to be certain for scenarios involving the use of nuclear weapons.

Acts of Terrorism
Political assassination escalates to war (assassin)
Mass murder attack and possible military retaliation (massmurder)

171

Electric power system sabotage and possible military retaliation (epsabotage)
Nuclear terrorist attack and possible military retaliation (nucdet)

The initiating event frequencies for all of the above terrorist attacks were based on my estimates. For each of the three non-nuclear initiators, I assumed a mean frequency of 0.05 per year (once in twenty years) with a triangular uncertainty distribution that ranged from 0.01 (once in ten years) to 0.02 (once in fifty years). For the relatively more difficult nuclear terrorist attack, I assumed a mean frequency of 0.005 per year (once in 200 years) with a lognormal uncertainty distribution that ranged up to a 95% value of 0.02 (once in 50 years).

All four of the terrorist acts listed above were modeled using the same event tree structure in the MFRA. The event tree structure contains two top event questions. The first question asks if societal life support systems (SLS) are maintained following the terrorist attack. This concern was judged to only be significant for the electric power sabotage and nuclear detonation attacks. The split fractions values used (SLSEP and SLSN) are my estimates. The second top event question allows for the likelihood of a military retaliation in response to the terrorist attack. The split fractions values used (ATTACKA, ATTACKMM, ATTACKEP, and ATTACKN) are my estimates.

Also remember from the war modeling discussion that the frequencies from the retaliation scenarios coming from these event trees are summed to form the *terrorwar* initiating event frequency. The *terrorwar* initiator is then evaluated with an event tree of the same structure used for armed conflict. The split fraction values used are changed to be appropriate for the different initiator. These split fraction values are summarized in Exhibit 17-6.

Biological Events & Accidents
Biological laboratory sabotage and possible military retaliation (biolabsab)
Biological weapon attack and possible military retaliation (bioattack)

Accidental release of known disease (bioaccident)

The initiating event frequencies for all of the above biological initiators were derived from the frequency estimated for a biological accident. I developed this frequency by assuming that an accidental biological release was most likely to originate from a biosafety level 4 (BSL-4) laboratory. Per reference 31 there are currently 42 such facilities worldwide. References #33 through #42 document how many precursor events have already occurred that narrowly missed producing serious consequences. And I am not using the term serious lightly. Per reference #36, "between 1978 and 1999, just over 1,200 people acquired infections from BSL-4 labs around the world; 22 were fatal. Since then, lab workers have been killed by Ebola and SARS, or severe acquired respiratory syndrome. Thieves tried to steal animal pathogens from an Indonesian lab in 2007." Based on this information I estimated a mean release frequency of 0.001 per year (once in a thousand years) for each facility. This yields a total release frequency of 0.042 per year. I then represented the uncertainty with a triangular distribution that ranged from 0.021 to 0.84 per year.

The initiating event frequencies for biological laboratory sabotage and biological attack were then established relative to the above derived frequency for accidental release. The key evidence I used to do this was reference #36. This Reuters article described safety and especially security requirements that I found appalling. Having spent nearly 40 years working in nuclear technology including serving as a Group Leader at Los Alamos National Laboratory, I have some familiarity with nuclear security requirements. After reading that the BSL-4 labs contain stores of deadly pathogens designated as "select agents" because they are fatal to humans and have no known vaccine or treatment, I expected to find nuclear class (or better) safety and security requirements in place. Not even close. In the United States, BSL-4 labs are located within high population areas (Atlanta) and, in at least one case, in an area with significant natural phenomena hazards (Galveston, Texas - hurricanes). Nuclear facilities would not be allowed in these locations. In addition, the operational security provisions described in reference #36 would only compare with those for the unclassified areas of Los Alamos.

The next step in my reasoning was that if potential bio terrorists were rational, they would take deadly pathogens from a BSL-4 facility and release them rather than bother producing their own. As a result, I set the biological laboratory sabotage (*biolabsab*) frequency equal to the accidental release frequency. Since I assumed that the pathogens used for biological attack (*bioattack*) were not stolen but independently produced, I set that frequency at one half the accidental release frequency.

All three of the biological initiators listed above were modeled using the same event tree structure in the MFRA. The event tree structure contains four top event questions. The first question asks if medical services capabilities are deliberately targeted as part of the initial attack. Obviously, if medical services are degraded, their ability to contain and mitigate the biological consequences of the attack will be reduced from normal conditions. The split fractions used (MEDOWNA and MEDOWNB) are my estimates. The second question queries the effectiveness of medical services in containing and mitigating the pathogen(s) released. For a biological accident event, the same split fraction (CFH) value used for a high severity natural pathogen was selected. This value was judged appropriate because even if the pathogen is not especially severe, medical services will respond robustly because they were the cause of the outbreak. For the biological laboratory sabotage and biological attack initiators, however, split fraction CFX was applied to medical services response capability and less credit was given for successful containment than for normally occurring outbreaks. The third of the event tree top event questions asks if societal life support systems (SLS) are maintained. The same split fraction values are used here as for normally occurring pandemics (SLSP). The final top event question asks if military retaliation is taken in response to the initiator. No retaliation is assumed for a biological accident but for biological laboratory sabotage or biological attack, a military response is assumed if the attack is successful in causing mass casualties in the target nation. If the attack is successfully contained, a military retaliation is still believed to be possible. The split fraction (ATTACKB) that allows for this possibility is my estimate.

Again remember from the war modeling discussion that the frequencies from the retaliation scenarios coming from these event trees are summed to form the *biowar* initiating event frequency. The *biowar* initiator is then evaluated with an event tree of the same structure used for armed conflict. The split fraction values used are changed to be appropriate for the different initiator. These split fraction values are summarized in the exhibit below.

Other Human Initiated Events & Accidents

International financial/economic crisis leads to government collapse & military conflict
References #55 & 60 give an overview of the role the United States has played in shaping the current global economy. As discussed earlier, the era of peace and prosperity experienced since World War II is unprecedented in human history. However, some other aspects of our time are also unprecedented. These include:

- A global financial and payments system that uses the U.S. dollar as the benchmark reserve currency.
- The worldwide use of fiat currencies with floating valuations, no nation today still employs a commodity (gold, silver, or oil) backed currency.
- The accumulation of record levels of both personal and sovereign debt.
- An ever increasing number of people living on government benefits rather than the fruits of their labor.
- The use of ever more complex financial engineering devices by corporations and governments.

175

Certainly we have experienced many financial panics and crises in modern history with at least two (1929 and 2008) being truly devastating. But we have always managed to repair the immediate problems, re-fire the economic engines, and move on without doing permanent damage to our society. But many are concerned that because of the above listed conditions, things might not go so well next time. The fundamental issue is this; the global financial system today is based on one thing, confidence. If anything should occur to shake that confidence, a devastating panic could result. Those most immediately affected by past panics were the rich who own assets that suffered sudden devaluation. Working class people who live mostly on current income are only affected if they lose jobs or find their wages eroded by runaway inflation. And these things take time to be realized. But because of the tens of millions now on welfare, any interruption or even threatened interruption of welfare payments will very quickly lead to severe unrest and violence. If not contained, this unrest could lead to the collapse and bankruptcy of governments. Because of the complex interdependencies that exist among governments and banks, a single important national bankruptcy could initiate a cascade effect similar to that which hit banks following the Lehman Brothers collapse in 2008. Such a global sovereign financial crisis has never been experienced. Possible resolution actions would be viewed by many people and governments as unacceptable (reference #43). There will be calls for military action to defend national interests and punish perceived wrong-doers. These events may spiral out of control into war.

The initiating event frequency for this event was based on data from reference #43. The international financial/economic crisis event tree structure contains two top event questions. The first question asks if the crisis is resolved without causing cascading government bankruptcies. The split fraction used (BROKE) is my estimate. The second top event question asks if the global economic restructuring that would be required following cascading national bankruptcies is successful without military action. The split fraction representing failure (BUST) is my estimate.

The frequency from event tree scenario #3 is assigned to the *crashwar* end state. The *crashwar* frequency is then evaluated with an event tree of the same structure used for armed conflict. The split fraction values used are changed to be appropriate for the different initiator. Note that for this initiator civil war is not modeled. This was done to avoid possible double counting between *crashwar* and *armcon*. It is very possible that the wars data used to develop the *armcon* frequency included civil conflicts caused by economic crises. The values used for other split fractions are summarized in the Exhibit below.

Exhibit 17-6 Split Fraction Values for War Event Trees

	Top Event	Scale of Conflict?			No nuclear EMP weapons used?	No other nuclear weapons used?			SLS systems maintained?	
	Split Fraction	CW	RW	GW	EMP	NWRW	NWGW	NWEMP	SLSCW	SLSRW
Event Tree	armcom	0.618	0.365	0.017	0.01	0.005	0.01	0.5	0.05	0.1
	biowar	0.0	0.5	0.1	0.05	0.005	0.01	0.5	n/a	0.1
	terrorwar	0.0	0.5	0.1	0.01	0.005	0.01	0.5	n/a	0.1
	crashwar	0.0	0.9	0.1	0.05	0.005	0.01	0.5	n/a	0.1

Chapter 18 - MEGA FATALITY CONSEQUENCE ASSESSMENT

The next step in the risk assessment process is to develop estimates of the prompt fatality consequences that would result from each of the scenarios evaluated in the MFRA. Determining how to do this presented a significant challenge. Most of the events modeled have never occurred or at least never occurred under conditions that would provide data useful to making prompt fatality estimates. Even for wars, the possible use of nuclear weapons against today's large populations could yield death tolls well beyond anything ever experienced.

So what could be done to estimate prompt fatalities given that there is no significant experience to build a data based model and also no "physics" model that I could imagine either? Some events like pandemics probably could be modeled mathematically, but this was beyond my capability and it wouldn't work for all scenarios. So after considerable thought, I elected to use a parametric approach using estimates for the population affected by the scenario and the percentage of the affected population that would be lost. In other words, I will use probability distributions to describe the uncertainty in consequences, but I will constrain the values that these distributions can take to credible estimates of the number of people that could be affected.

To make prompt fatality estimates in a consistent manner, I built the lethality matrix shown in the next exhibit. The rows of this matrix define nine population ranges or categories and the columns specify lethality fractions. The cells of the matrix contain the resulting products of the mean population and lethality fraction at each intersection. The values range from the smallest at the upper left (500) to the largest (7 billion) at the lower right. The rows (P1-9) and columns (L1-9) are labeled so that each of the 81 cells can be identified by label (P1L1 thru P9L9). I then made prompt fatality consequence estimates for each end state in the MFRA by selecting first a representative affected population and then choosing what I judged to be a reasonable lethality fraction. In most cases, I let the number of deaths indicated in the selected cell of the lethality matrix be the mean value of a lognormal distribution. To allow for uncertainty, I then chose a second cell with a greater population and/or a higher lethality fraction and assigned this higher number to the 95th or 99th percentile. The cells chosen for each end state are indicated in the end state data table in Chapter 20. For end states that included failure of societal life support systems (SLS) I made what I believe to be reasonable selections for both the population affected and the lethality fraction.

To help illustrate the resulting fatality estimates, I reproduced the lethality matrix structure in Exhibit 18-2 and then posted each end state code in the cell of the lethality matrix that best represented the calculated mean value of each end state distribution. Note that the mean values do not generally fall in the lower right region of the lethality matrix because of the large uncertainty included in these estimates. If I had allowed the mean values to become too great, then the higher percentile values of the distributions could exceed the total population of humans. Thus, I had to exercise care in constructing the distributions for the more severe events to be sure that the higher percentiles above the mean value did not exceed the maximum possible population.

Although this process for modeling consequences is based on my judgment and expertise, I believe the resulting distributions for prompt fatalities are reasonable and reflect a level of uncertainty commensurate with the approximate nature of the approach. Admittedly, a more rigorous estimating method would be desirable. However, I found no benchmarks in historical data or predictive analysis that could be applied to this question. A more rigorous approach for estimating the consequences to a modern industrialized society from prolonged electric power outages or other SLS breakdowns would be especially valuable to this and many other analyses.

Exhibit 18-1 Lethality Matrix

Population Affected (millions)		Mean Lethality									
Range	mean	1.0E-04	1.E-03	1.E-02	0.1	0.3	0.5	0.8	0.9	1.0	
0-10	5.00E+06	5.0E+02	5.0E+03	5.0E+04	5.0E+05	1.3E+06	2.5E+06	3.8E+06	4.5E+06	5.0E+06	P1
10-50	3.00E+07	3.0E+03	3.0E+04	3.0E+05	3.0E+06	7.5E+06	1.5E+07	2.3E+07	2.7E+07	3.0E+07	P2
50-100	7.50E+07	7.5E+03	7.5E+04	7.5E+05	7.5E+06	1.9E+07	3.8E+07	5.6E+07	6.8E+07	7.5E+07	P3
100-500	3.00E+08	3.0E+04	3.0E+05	3.0E+06	3.0E+07	7.5E+07	1.5E+08	2.3E+08	2.7E+08	3.0E+08	P4
500-1000	7.50E+08	7.5E+04	7.5E+05	7.5E+06	7.5E+07	1.9E+08	3.8E+08	5.6E+08	6.8E+08	7.5E+08	P5
1000-3000	2.00E+09	2.0E+05	2.0E+06	2.0E+07	2.0E+08	5.0E+08	1.0E+09	1.5E+09	1.8E+09	2.0E+09	P6
3000-5000	4.00E+09	4.0E+05	4.0E+06	4.0E+07	4.0E+08	1.0E+09	2.0E+09	3.0E+09	3.6E+09	4.0E+09	P7
5000-7000	6.00E+09	6.0E+05	6.0E+06	6.0E+07	6.0E+08	1.5E+09	3.0E+09	4.5E+09	5.4E+09	6.0E+09	P8
7000	7.00E+09	7.0E+05	7.0E+06	7.0E+07	7.0E+08	1.8E+09	3.5E+09	5.3E+09	6.3E+09	7.0E+09	P9
		L1	L2	L3	L4	L5	L6	L7	L8	L9	

Exhibit 18-2 Mapping of End State Mean Value Fatalities to the Lethality Matrix

	Population Affected (millions)		Mean Lethality								
	Range	mean	1.0E-04	1.E-03	1.E-02	0.1	0.3	0.5	0.8	0.9	1.0
			L1	L2	L3	L4	L5	L6	L7	L8	L9
P1	0-10	5.00E+06					PF10m		nucattack		nucattack+
P2	10-50	3.00E+07		wardths1	wardths2	equake chaos1	flood PF100m				
P3	50-100	7.50E+07					PF100m+				
P4	100-500	3.00E+08		wardths3		chaos2					
P5	500-1000	7.50E+08		pand2	pand3						
P6	1000-3000	2.00E+09	pand1	wardths4	pand3+	wardths8 chaos3	PF1km				
P7	3000-5000	4.00E+09		pand4		wardths7 pand5	PF1km+				
P8	5000-7000	6.00E+09		wardths6	wardths5		wardths9 pand5+				
P9	7000	7.00E+09				chaos4	PF10km				

Chapter 19 - MEGA FATALITY RISK ASSESSMENT RESULTS

Now we are ready to take a look at the results of our risk assessment model. Let's begin at the total expected risk for mega fatalities. The next exhibit shows the distribution calculated by Crystal Ball for our top level result of mean expected prompt fatalities per year (PF/yr).

Exhibit 19-1 Total MFRA Expected Fatalities per year

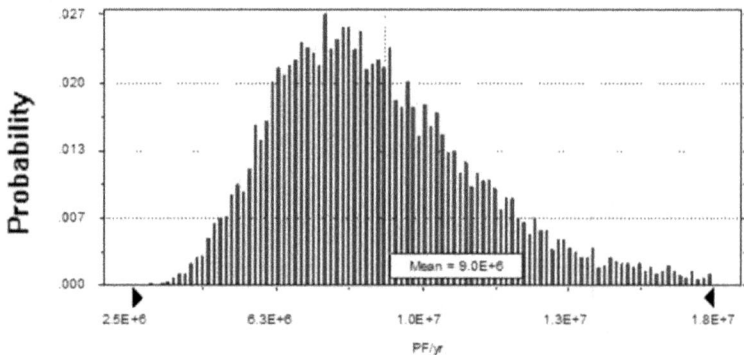

For a population of 7.2 billion people, this level of fatalities (9.0E6 per year) represents an individual risk of 1.25E-3 per year. Let's consider the reasonableness of this result. From the data on human fatalities I discussed in Chapter 15, we know that the actual fatality risk from all causes is about 8E-3 per year. So our risk assessment results say that mega-fatality events represent about 15% of the existing risk we face from all causes. This statement is actually a bit of an exaggeration because, as you may have noticed, I included data on all epidemics and all wars in determining the initiating event frequencies for the MFRA. I then let the modelling process determine what fraction of these initiators actually produced mega-fatality scenarios. That means that some non-mega fatality scenarios are also included in our total analysis results. In building the MFRA risk model, I thought this was a conservative approach and would avoid having to sort out the less severe scenarios. But since actual deaths from epidemics and wars are also included in the historical data, it does mean that just adding 1.25E-3 to the historical 8E-3 would be double counting some events. But even after acknowledging this issue, I think the overall result passes the ho-ho test for reasonableness. So now let's look at what the risk assessment results tell us about contributors.

Initiating Events

The exhibit below shows how the initiating events ranked in order of importance. Importance is calculated by setting each initiator equal to zero and recording the change in total risk. In other words, the percentages indicate how much the total risk would be reduced if that initiator could be totally eliminated. The importance column shows where to focus risk reduction actions in order to produce the most effect on risk results.

Exhibit 19-2   MFRA Initiating Events Ranked by Importance

Code	Description	calculated Mean	Importance
armcon	Conventional armed conflict	3.0E+00	31.1%
NatEpid	Natural Epidemic	3.7E+00	28.9%
biolabsab	Biological laboratory sabotage	4.9E-02	11.1%
SolStrm	Solar Storm	1.2E-02	9.3%
epsabotage	Electric power system sabotage	5.7E-02	8.5%
bioattack	Biological weapon attack	2.4E-02	5.5%
crash	International financial/economic crisis	9.1E-02	3.1%
Mquake	Mega Earthquake	8.6E-01	1.3%
nucdet	Nuclear terrorist attack	7.1E-03	0.7%

End States

The next exhibit shows the risk ranking for each of the end states. Since each scenario terminates into a specific end state, the risk ranking here is just the percentage contribution of each end state to the total risk. This result also helps show where to focus risk reduction actions in order to produce the most effect on risk results.

Exhibit 19-3   MFRA End States Ranked by Contribution to Risk

End State	Description	Percent Rank
pand3+	Epidemic of medium severity w/o effective containment + regional SLS breakdown	16.3%
wardths9	Global nuclear war + global SLS failure	15.1%
pand5+	Pandemic of high severity w/o effective containment + global SLS breakdown	10.9%
chaos3	Societal life support system (SLS) failure impacting 1 billion people	8.9%
chaos2	Societal life support system (SLS) failure impacting 100 million people	7.8%
wardths6	Global conventional war + regional SLS failure	7.8%
wardths5	Regional nuclear war + regional SLS failure	7.2%
wardths7	Global nuclear war + regional SLS failure	3.9%
wardths3	Regional conventional war	3.7%
pand1	Epidemic of low severity w/o effective containment	3.1%

Scenario Level Results

Now let's look at the results for the individual scenarios. The next exhibit lists the top twelve scenarios by contribution to total risk.

Exhibit 19-4 Model Scenarios Ranked by Contribution to Risk

Scenario #	Scenario Description	Frequency (events/yr)	End State	Risk (PF/yr)	Risk Rank (%)
Natepid8	Pandemic of high severity w/o effective containment + global SLS breakdown	1.2E-03	pand5+	9.8E+05	10.9%
SolStrm3	Solar storm w extended electric power outage &regional SLS failure	7.4E-03	chaos3	8.0E+05	8.9%
armcon9	Global nuclear war + global SLS failure	5.7E-04	wardths9	7.8E+05	8.7%
biolabsab5	Pandemic + regional SLS failure + retaliation attack	3.9E-02	pand3+	5.8E+05	6.4%
armcon5	Regional nuclear war + regional SLS failure	9.5E-03	wardths5	5.7E+05	6.3%
Natepid5	Epidemic of medium severity w/o effective containment + regional SLS breakdown	3.7E-02	pand3+	5.5E+05	6.1%
armcon6	Global conventional war + regional SLS failure	5.1E-02	wardths6	5.0E+05	5.6%
epsabotage4	Electric power system sabotage with regional SLS failure + armed conflict	2.10E-02	chaos2	4.9E+05	5.5%
biowar9	Global nuclear war + global SLS failure	2.60E-04	wardths9	3.5E+05	3.9%
armcon3	Regional conventional war	9.60E-01	wardths3	2.9E+05	3.2%
bioattack5	Epidemic of medium severity w/o effective containment + regional SLS breakdown	1.90E-02	pand3+	2.8E+05	3.1%
Natepid2	Epidemic of low severity w/o effective containment	1.6E+00	pand1	2.8E+05	3.1%

Now is also an appropriate time to view the mean risk curve described by these results.

Exhibit 19-5 Mean Risk Curve for MFRA

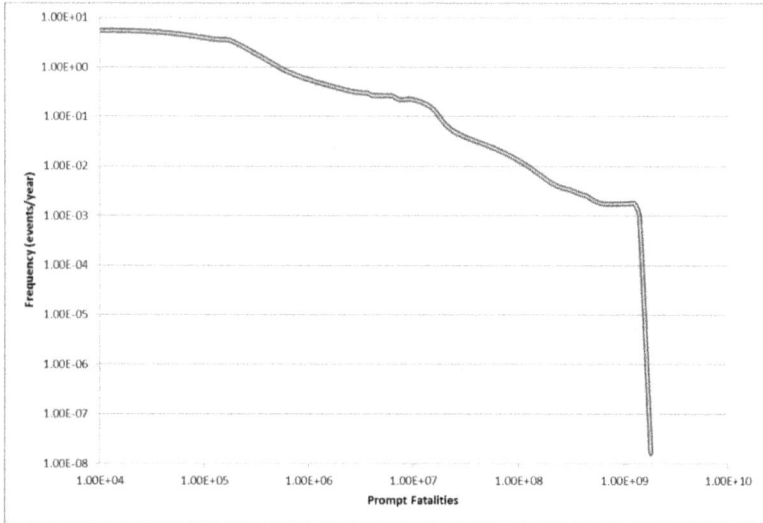

Note that the risk curve falls off very sharply at a frequency of about 1 E-3. This is because the risk model predicts that wars, pandemics, and other events can do a pretty good job of killing us all off at quite high frequencies. There is no need to wait for asteroids or aliens. As a result, the frequency screen of 1 E-8 (based on a 10km asteroid strike) that I used earlier turned out to be very, very conservative. If I cut off the risk curve at 1 E-4 (a factor of 10,000 higher) I can get a better view of the contributors without losing any important information. In the next exhibit I have done this and added the highest ranking scenarios from Exhibit 19-4.

Exhibit 19-6 Truncated Mean Risk Curve with Key Scenarios

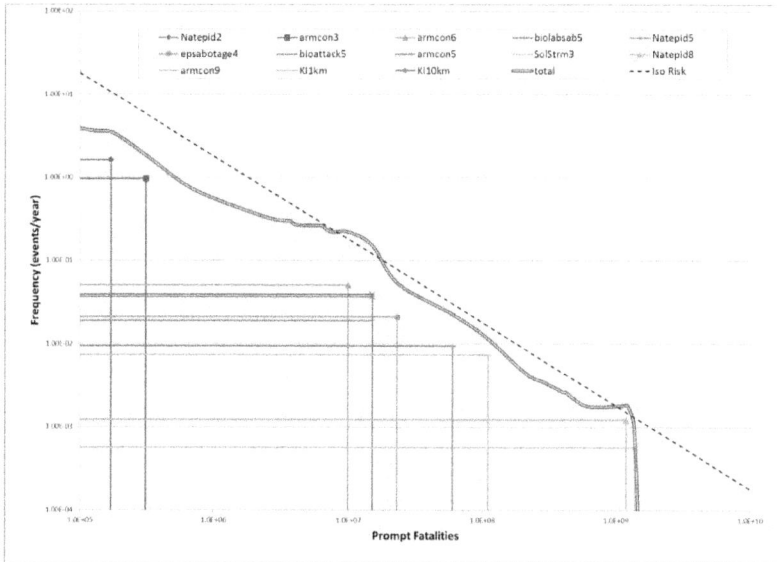

Discussion of Results

Now that you have had a chance to see and think about the MFRA risk assessment quantitative results, let's look at what they might mean. The following are what I believe to be the key findings of this risk assessment.

- Mega fatality risk was found to be dominated by three categories of events; disease, wars, and prolonged electric power system outages. The first two have always been known to us and are constantly in the focus of our attention. Potential massive and long lasting electric power system failures are a byproduct of modern civilization and a new threat that has almost no one's attention.

- A possible reason why electric power system outages have not received adequate attention is because they can emanate from three quite distinct threats: solar storms, direct sabotage, and nuclear EMP weapon use. To develop effective risk reduction actions, all threats will need to be considered.

- In addition to electric power system sabotage, the most significant terrorist threat was found to come from the deliberate release of special agents from BSL-4 laboratories. I found the large number of these facilities (42) combined with their locations near high population zones and questionable safety and security provisions to represent a clear and present danger that should be immediately reviewed.

- Terrorism in all forms was found to represent not only a direct threat to cause mega fatality events but is also a potentially important initiator of future wars.

- Natural epidemics combined with potential biological accidents and deliberate terrorists acts make biological events the highest ranking general category of threat found in the MFRA.

- Among events that are considered "acts of God" only solar storms made a significant contribution to the overall risk results.

- Although not a large contributor, another scenario of interest appearing in the results was *crashwar*. This is an armed conflict initiated by an international financial crisis. This represents another new threat presented by modern global civilization that deserves further attention.

- Because of our ever increasing dependence on modern technologies to supply basic human needs, the loss of human life was found to be significantly increased in scenarios that included the prolonged disruption of these societal life support systems (SLS). The dynamics of potential SLS failures and the identification of possible risk reduction actions is a subject that deserves immediate and extensive study.

Final Comments

I could provide much more documentation and discussion of the MFRA, but it was not my objective to produce the ultimate analysis of mega fatality risk. I deliberately kept the MFRA risk model relatively simple (67 scenarios), used commercially available software, and relied only on publically available information. This was an exercise meant to demonstrate that the risk assessment methods and tools I dragged you through in Parts II and III are not just theoretical toys. They can actually be applied to real world problems. I picked the subject of mega fatality risk because I thought it would be of interest to almost everyone. I had never thought about it seriously before this project.

As you can see by inspection of the actual model in the next chapter, the MFRA risk model contains many subjective judgments (I warned you). Reasonable people with better information may find reasons to disagree with the decisions I made in constructing the MFRA. This could produce different results. Also, a dedicated team of risk analysts and subject matter experts using more sophisticated software and non-publically available information could produce a much more rigorous risk assessment. Based on the significance of my results, this probably should be done. But whether or not a more rigorous analysis would produce dramatically different conclusions is a question I will leave to you.

As for the objective of demonstrating the power of quantitative risk analysis, if you can say that your knowledge of mega fatality risk has been improved (maybe a lot) by reading my analysis, the mission has been accomplished.

Chapter 20 - MFRA EXCEL/CRYSTAL BALL MODEL

The following pages are taken directly from the Crystal Ball/Excel file built for the MFRA risk model. I apologize for small size of the print on some pages. If you are interested in examining the model in greater detail, please go to *jpkindinger.com* where you can download a PDF file containing a larger version of these pages.

Initiating Event Data

	Initiator		Distribution								Source References
Code	Description	Form	%tile	Value	%tile	Value	%tile	Value	calculated Mean	
Cosmic Events											
KI10m	Kinetic Impact of 10 m object	T	0	0.01	50	0.1	100	0.25	1.2E-01	Reference #1 & 2
KI100m	Kinetic Impact of 100 m object	LN	mean	2.E-04	95	1.0E-03			3.E-04	Reference #1 & 2
KI1km	Kinetic Impact of 1 km object	LN	mean	2.E-06	95	1.0E-05			3.E-06	Reference #1 & 2
KI10km	Kinetic Impact of 10 km object	LN	mean	1.E-08	95	5.0E-08			2.E-08	Reference #1 & 2
SolStrm	Solar Storm	LN	mean	1.2E-02	95	1.0E-03			1.21E-02	Reference #13
Natural Terrestrial Events											
SuperV7	VEI category 7 volcanic eruption	LN	mean	1.8E-06	99	1.8E-05			2.9E-06	estimated 22 events in 12 million years, Reference #4
SuperV8	VEI category 8 volcanic eruption	LN	mean	3.3E-07	99	3.3E-06			5.4E-07	estimated 10 events in 30 million years, Reference #4
Mquake	Mega Earthquake	LN	mean	7.9E-01	95	1.6E+00			8.7E-01	89 events recorded in 113 years, Reference #6
Mflood	Other flood event	LN	mean	3.0E-03	95	6.0E-03			3.3E-03	3 events in 1000 years, Reference #7
NatEpid	Natural Epidemic	T	0	2	50	4	100	5	3.671014	42 events in 10 years, Reference #26
Agression by Nation States											
armcon	Conventional armed conflict	T	0	1	50	3.09	100	5	3.03	173 wars in 56 years, References #53 & 54
biowar	War in retaliation for terror attack								7.3E-02	from biological event trees
terrorwar	War in retaliation for biological attack								5.3E-02	from terror event trees
crashwar	War following economic collapse								3.3E-02	from economic crash event tree
Acts of Terrorism											
assassin	Political assassination	T	0	0.02	50	0.05	100	0.1	5.6E-02	estimated base rate of 1 in 20 years
massmurder	Mass murder attack	T	0	0.02	50	0.05	100	0.1	5.6E-02	estimated base rate of 1 in 20 years
epsabotage	Electric power system sabotage	T	0	0.02	50	0.05	100	0.1	5.7E-02	estimated base rate of 1 in 20 years
nucdet	Nuclear terrorist attack	LN	mean	0.005	95	0.02			7.1E-02	estimated base rate of 1 in 200 years
bioattack	Biological weapon attack	T	0	0.01	50	0.021	100	0.04	2.4E-02	1/2 the accidental release risk for BSL-4 labs
biolabsab	Biological laboratory sabotage	T	0	0.021	50	0.042	100	0.084	4.9E-02	Equals the accidental release risk for BSL-4 labs
Other Human Initiated Events & Accidents											
bioaccident	Accidental release of known disease	T	0	0.021	50	0.042	100	0.084	4.9E-02	42 BSL-4 labs world wide @ 1E-3/yr per lab
crash	International financial/economic crisis	T	0	0.041	50	0.091	100	0.141	9.1E-02	Reference #43 Figure 1

Split Fraction Data

Code	Description	Form	%ile	Value	%ile	Value	%ile	Value	calculated Mean	Source References
	Initiator				Distribution					
HPZ	Probability of impact in high population zone	T	0	0.01	50	0.02	100	0.05	0.027	550 cities w > 1M people, a hit within a 50 mi radius of each gives a target of 4.3 mil sq mi or ~ 2%
PSH	Probability that pathogen severity is high	T	0	0.001	50	0.005	100	0.01	0.009	JPK analysis of ref 26 data
PSM	Probability that pathogen severity is medium	T	0	0.05	50	0.1	100	0.15	0.100	JPK analysis of ref 26 data
CFL	Containment failure for low severity pathogen	T	0	0.25	50	0.5	100	0.75	0.500	JPK estimate
CFM	Containment failure for medium severity pathogen	T	0	0.1	50	0.2	100	0.3	0.200	JPK estimate
CFH	Containment failure for high severity pathogen	T	0	0.025	50	0.05	100	0.075	0.050	JPK estimate
CFX	Containment failure following terrorist attack	T	0	0.2	50	0.25	100	0.5	0.316	JPK estimate
MEDOWNA	Medical services disrupted by bio lab sabotage	T	0	0.6	50	0.8	100	1	0.799	JPK estimate
MEDOWNB	Medical services disrupted by bio attack	T	0	0.05	50	0.1	100	0.25	0.133	JPK estimate
SLSND	Failure of SLS systems following natural disaster	T	0	0.6	50	0.8	100	1	0.798	JPK estimate
SLSP	Failure of SLS systems during pandemic	T	0	0.25	50	0.5	100	0.75	0.500	JPK estimate
SLSEP	Failure of SLS systems during extended EP outage	T	0	0.25	50	0.5	100	0.75	0.499	JPK estimate
SLSND	Failure of SLS systems following nuclear detonation	T	0	0.25	50	0.5	100	0.75	0.499	JPK estimate
SLSCW	Failure of SLS systems in a civil war	T	0	0.02	50	0.05	100	0.2	0.090	JPK estimate
SLSRW	Failure of SLS systems in a regional war	T	0	0.05	50	0.1	100	0.25	0.134	JPK estimate
EPR	EP recovery failure following solar storm	T	0	0.5	50	0.8	100	1	0.766	JPK estimate
ATTACKB	Retaliation following bio attack	T	0	0.25	50	0.5	100	0.75	0.499	JPK estimate
ATTACKA	Retaliation following assassination	T	0	0.01	50	0.05	100	0.2	0.086	JPK estimate
ATTACKMM	Retaliation following mass murder	T	0	0.1	50	0.25	100	0.4	0.250	JPK estimate
ATTACKEP	Retaliation following EP system attack	T	0	0.5	50	0.75	100	1	0.750	JPK estimate
ATTACKN	Retaliation following nuclear attack	T	0	0.5	50	0.9	100	1	0.800	JPK estimate
BROKE	Failure to avoid cascading bankruptcies after a crash	T	0	0.25	50	0.5	100	0.75	0.500	JPK estimate
BUST	Failure to restructure economies after bankruptcy	T	0	0.1	50	0.2	100	0.5	0.266	JPK estimate
GWAC	Probability armed conflict becomes global war	T	0	0.010	50	0.017	100	0.025	0.017	3/173 wars per references 53 & 54
GWTW	Probability terror war becomes global war	T	0	0.050	50	0.100	100	0.250	0.133	JPK estimate
RWAC	Probability armed conflict becomes regional war	T	0	0.250	50	0.365	100	0.480	0.364	63/173 wars per references 53 &54
EMPAC	EMP weapon used during armed conflict	T	0	0.005	50	0.010	100	0.050	0.022	JPK estimate
EMPBW	EMP weapon used during bio war	T	0	0.010	50	0.050	100	0.100	0.053	JPK estimate
EMPTW	EMP weapon used during terror retaliation	T	0	0.005	50	0.010	100	0.020	0.012	JPK estimate
EMPCW	EMP weapon used during economic crash war	T	0	0.010	50	0.050	100	0.100	0.053	JPK estimate
NWRW	Nuclear weapons used in a regional war	T	0	0.001	50	0.005	100	0.020	0.009	JPK estimate
NWGW	Nuclear weapons used in a global war	T	0	0.005	50	0.010	100	0.020	0.012	JPK estimate
NWEMP	Nuclear weapons used after EMP	T	0	0.250	50	0.500	100	0.750	0.501	JPK estimate

Risk Management Revisited

End State Data

	End State Data		Distribution (fatalities)									calculated Mean
Code	Description	Form	%tile	Value	LM Ref	%tile	Value	LM Ref	%tile	Value	LM Ref	
nomega	Not a mega fatality scenario											
PF10m	Fatalities from 10 m impact on high population zone	LN	mean	5.0E+05	P1L4	95	4.5E+06	P1L8				1.2E+06
PF100m	Fatalities from 100 m impact	LN	mean	3.0E+06	P2L4	95	2.7E+07	P2L8				7.4E+06
PF100mp	Fatalities from 100 m impact + local SLS breakdown	LN	mean	8.0E+06	P3L4	95	6.8E+07	P3L8				1.9E+07
PF1km	Fatalities from 1 km impact	LN	mean	2.0E+08	P6L4	95	1.5E+09	P6L7				4.1E+08
PF1kmp	Fatalities from 1 km impact + regional SLS breakdown	LN	mean	5.0E+08	P6L5	99	2.0E+09	P6L9				6.0E+08
PF10km	Fatalities from 10 km impact	LN	mean	1.5E+09	P8L5	99	6.0E+09	P8L9				1.8E+09
chaos1	10 million affected by SLS failure	LN	mean	3.0E+06	P2L4	95	7.5E+06	P2L5				3.5E+06
chaos2	100 million affected by SLS failure	LN	mean	1.9E+07	P3L5	95	5.6E+07	P3L7				2.3E+07
chaos3	1 billion affected by SLS failure	LN	mean	7.5E+07	P5L4	99	5.6E+08	P5L7				1.1E+08
chaos4	7 billion affected by SLS failure	LN	mean	7.0E+08	P9L4	99	6.3E+09	P9L8				1.1E+09
equake	direct fatalities + local chaos	T	0	5.0E+03	P1L2	50	3.0E+05	P2L3	100	7.5E+06	P3L4	2.6E+06
flood	direct fatalities + local chaos	T	0	5.0E+05	P1L4	50	1.3E+06	P2L5	100	1.5E+07	P2L6	5.7E+06
pand1	low severity w/o effective containment	LN	5	7.0E+03	P3L1	95	6.0E+05	P6L1				1.7E+05
pand2	medium severity w effective containment	LN	5	7.5E+04	P3L2	95	2.0E+06	P6L2				6.4E+05
pand3	medium severity w/o effective containment	LN	5	7.5E+05	P3L3	95	2.0E+07	P6L3				6.3E+06
pand3p	medium severity w/o effective containment + regional SLS breakdown	LN	5	3.0E+06	P4L3	95	4.0E+07	P7L3				1.5E+07
pand4	high severity w effective containment	LN	5	2.0E+06	P6L2	95	6.0E+06	P8L2				3.7E+06
pand5	high severity w/o effective containment	LN	5	4.0E+07	P7L3	95	1.0E+09	P7L5				3.0E+08
pand5p	high severity w/o effective containment + global SLS breakdown	LN	50	1.0E+09	P7L5	99	4.5E+09	P8L7				1.2E+09
nucattack	nuclear detonation in high population area	LN	mean	1.3E+06	P1L5	95	1.5E+07	P2L6				4.0E+06
nucattackp	nuclear detonation in high population area + local SLS breakdown	LN	mean	2.5E+06	P1L6	95	2.3E+07	P2L7				6.4E+06
wardths1	Civil war	LN	5	5.0E+03	P1L2	95	5.0E+04	P1L3				2.0E+04
wardths2	Civil war + local SLS failure	LN	5	3.0E+04	P2L2	95	3.0E+05	P2L3				1.2E+05
wardths3	Regional conventional war	LN	5	7.5E+04	P3L2	95	7.5E+05	P3L3				3.1E+05
wardths4	Regional conventional war + local SLS failure	LN	5	3.0E+05	P4L2	95	3.0E+06	P4L3				1.2E+06
wardths5	Regional nuclear war + regional SLS failure	LN	5	7.5E+06	P5L3	95	1.9E+08	P5L5				6.0E+07
wardths6	Global conventional war + regional SLS failure	LN	5	2.0E+06	P6L2	90	2.0E+07	P6L4				9.9E+06
wardths7	Global nuclear war + regional SLS failure	LN	5	2.0E+08	P6L4	99	1.0E+09	P6L6				4.2E+08
wardths8	Global conventional war + global SLS failure	LN	5	4.0E+07	P7L3	99	1.0E+09	P7L5				2.1E+08
wardths9	Global nuclear war + global SLS failure	LN	5	6.0E+08	P8L4	99	3.5E+09	P9L6				1.4E+09

LM Ref = reference cell from leathality matrix

Risk Management Revisited

PAGE 4

Kinetic Impacts Event Trees

Initiator	Impact in low population area?	#	Frequency (events/yr)	End State	Risk (PF/yr)	Comments
KI10m	Yes	1	1.2E-01	nomega		
	HPZ	2	3.2E-03	PF10m	3.9E+03	

Initiator	SLS systems maintained?	#	Frequency (events/yr)	End State	Risk (PF/yr)	Comments
KI100m	Yes	1	6.5E-05	PF100m	4.8E+02	
	SLSND	2	2.6E-04	PF100mp	4.9E+03	PF100m + local SLS failure

Initiator	SLS systems maintained?	#	Frequency (events/yr)	End State	Risk (PF/yr)	Comments
KI1km	Yes	1	6.4E-07	PF1km	2.6E+02	
	SLSND	2	2.5E-06	PF1kmp	1.5E+03	PF1km + regional SLS failure

Initiator	SLS systems maintained?	#	Frequency (events/yr)	End State	Risk (PF/yr)	Comments
KI10km	GNo	1	1.6E-08	PF10km	2.9E+01	

4.6E+03 Total Kinetic Impact Risk

Natural Terrestrial Event Trees

Super Volcano events

Initiator	SLS systems maintained?	#	Frequency (events/yr)	End State	Risk (PF/yr)	Comments
SuperV7	Yes	1	5.8E-07	chaos1	2.1E+00	breakdown of SLS systems - local SLS failure
	SLSND	2	2.3E-06	chaos2	5.4E+01	breakdown of SLS systems - regional SLS failure

Initiator	SLS systems maintained?	#	Frequency (events/yr)	End State	Risk (PF/yr)	Comments
SuperV8	Yes	1	1.1E-07	chaos3	1.2E+01	breakdown of SLS systems - regional SLS failure
	SLSND	2	4.3E-07	chaos4	4.6E+02	breakdown of SLS systems - global SLS failure

5.3E+02 Total Volcano Risk

Mega Earthquake

Initiator	Impact in low population area?	#	Frequency (events/yr)	End State	Risk (PF/yr)	Comments
Mquake	Yes	1	8.5E-01	nomega		
	HPZ	2	2.3E-02	equake	6.0E+04	direct fatalities + local SLS failure

Mega Flood

Initiator	Impact in low population area?	#	Frequency (events/yr)	End State	Risk (PF/yr)	Comments
Mflood	GNo	1	3.3E-03	flood	1.9E+04	direct fatalities + local SLS failure

Solar Storm

Initiator	Successful EP system recovery?	SLS systems maintained?	#	Frequency (events/yr)	End State	Risk (PF/yr)	Comments
SolStrm	N/A	GS	1	2.8E-03	nomega	5.1E+06	successful recovery
	EPR		2	1.9E-03	chaos2	4.4E+04	prolonged electric power outage + local SLS failure
		SLSND	3	7.4E-03	chaos3	8.0E+05	breakdown of SLS systems - regional SLS failure

1.2E-02   5.9E+06 Total solar storm risk

Risk Management Revisited

Natural Epidemics Event Tree

Initiator	Pathogen Severity Level?	Med Services Effective?	SLS Systems Maintained?	#	Frequency (events/yr)	End State	Risk (PF/yr)	Comments
Natepid	Low	Yes	GYes	1	1.67E+00	nomega		low severity w effective containment
		CFL	GYes	2	1.64E+00	pand1	2.81E+05	low severity w/o effective containment
	Medium (PSM)	Yes	GYes	3	2.94E-01	pand2	1.88E+05	medium severity w effective containment
		CFM	GYes	4	3.68E-02	pand3	2.33E+05	medium severity w/o effective containment
			SLSP	5	3.68E-02	pand3+	5.48E+05	medium severity w/o effective containment + regional SLS bre:
	High (PSH)	Yes	GYes	6	3.04E-02	pand4	1.11E+05	high severity w effective containment
		CFH	Yes	7	7.97E-04	pand5	2.36E+05	high severity w/o effective containment
			SLSP	8	7.96E-04	pand5+	9.81E+05	high severity w/o effective containment + global SLS breakdow
					3.71E+00		2.58E+06	Total epidemics risk

Other Biological Event Trees

Initiator	Med services not attacked?	Med Services Effective?	SLS systems maintained?	Retaliation attack?	#	Frequency (events/yr)	End State	Risk (PF/yr)	Comments
bioaccident	GYes	Yes	GYes	N/A	1	4.63E-02	nomega		successful recovery
		CFH	Yes	N/A	2	1.21E-03	pand3	7.68E+03	pandemic
			SLSP	N/A	3	1.21E-03	pand3+	1.81E+04	pandemic + local SLS failure
						4.87E-02		2.58E+04	Total bioaccident risk

Initiator	Med services not attacked?	Med Services Effective?	SLS systems maintained?	Retaliation attack?	#	Frequency (events/yr)	End State	Risk (PF/yr)	Comments
biolabsab	Yes	Yes	GYes	No	1	0.0E+00	nomega		peaceful recovery
				ATTACKB	2	6.7E-03	nomega		successful recovery + retaliation attack
		CFX	Yes	GYes	3	1.6E-03	pand3	9.8E+03	pandemic + retaliation attack
			SLSP	GYes	4	1.6E-03	pand3+	2.3E+04	pandemic + regional SLS failure + retal
	MEDOWNA	GNo	GNo	GYes	5	3.9E-02	pand3+	5.8E+05	pandemic + regional SLS failure + retal
						4.9E-02		6.1E+05	Total bio lab sabotage risk

Initiator	Med services not attacked?	Med Services Effective?	SLS systems maintained?	Retaliation attack?	#	Frequency (events/yr)	End State	Risk (PF/yr)	Comments
bioattack	Yes	Yes	GYes	No	1	0.0E+00	nomega		pandemic
				ATTACKB	2	3.3E-03	nomega		successful recovery + retaliation attack
		CFX	Yes	GYes	3	7.5E-04	pand3	4.8E+03	pandemic + retaliation attack
			SLSP	GYes	4	7.5E-04	pand3+	1.1E+04	pandemic + regional SLS failure + retal
	MEDOWNB	GNo	GNo	GYes	5	1.9E-02	pand3+	2.8E+05	pandemic + regional SLS failure + retal
						2.4E-02		3.0E+05	Total bio attack risk

7.26E-02   biowar   total frequency for bio retaliation attack

197

Terrorism Event Trees

Initiator	SLS systems maintained?	No military retaliation?	#	Frequency (events/yr)	End State	Risk (PF/yr)	Comments
assassin	GYes	Yes	1	5.16E-02	nomega		Peaceful recovery
		ATTACKA	2	4.88E-03	terrorwar		Military retaliation for assination

Initiator	SLS systems maintained?	No military retaliation?	#	Frequency (events/yr)	End State	Risk (PF/yr)	Comments
massmurder	GYes	Yes	1	4.24E-02	nomega		Peaceful recovery
		ATTACKMM	2	1.41E-02	terrorwar		Military retaliation for mass murder

Initiator	SLS systems maintained?	No military retaliation?	#	Frequency (events/yr)	End State	Risk (PF/yr)	Comments
epsabotage	Yes	Yes	1	2.13E-02	nomega	n/a	Peaceful recovery
		ATTACKEP	2	7.09E-03	terrorwar	n/a	Military retaliation for EP sabotage
	SLSEP	Yes	3	7.05E-03	chaos2	1.64E+05	Regional SLS failure w/o armed conflict
		ATTACKEP	4	2.12E-02	chaos2	4.94E+05	Regional SLS failure + armed conflict
				5.66E-02		6.58E+05	Total EP sabotage risk

Initiator	SLS systems maintained?	No military retaliation?	#	Frequency (events/yr)	End State	Risk (PF/yr)	Comments
nucdet	Yes	Yes	1	2.87E-04	nucattack	1.16E+03	Peaceful recovery
		ATTACKN	2	1.15E-03	nucattack	4.64E+03	Military retaliation for nuclear atack
	SLSND	Yes	3	1.14E-03	nucattackp	7.27E+03	Chaos w/o retaliation
		ATTACKN	4	4.56E-03	nucattackp	2.92E+04	Chaos with retaliation
				7.13E-03		4.22E+04	Total nuclear detonation risk

International financial/economic crisis Event Tree

Initiator	Cascading government bankruptcies avoided?	Economic restructuring w/o conflict?	#	Frequency (events/yr)	End State	Risk (PF/yr)	Comments
crash	Yes	N/A	1	4.56E-02	nomega	n/a	Peaceful recovery
	BROKE	Yes	2	1.21E-02	nomega	n/a	Peaceful recovery
		BUST	3	3.34E-02	crashwar	n/a	Armed conflict, global war w nuclear nations (crashwar)

WAR EVENT TREES

Initiator	Scale of Conflict?	No nuclear EMP weapons used?	No other nuclear weapons used?	SLS systems maintained?	#	Frequency (events/yr)	End State	Risk (PF/yr)	Comments
armcon	Civil War (CW)	GYes	GYes	Yes	1	1.7E+00	wardths1	3.5E+04	Civil war
				SLSCW	2	1.7E-01	wardths2	2.1E+04	Civil war + local SLS failure
	Regional War (RWAC)	GYes	GYes	Yes	3	9.6E-01	wardths3	2.9E+05	Regional conventional war
				SLSRW	4	1.5E-01	wardths4	1.8E+05	Regional conventional war + local SLS failure
			NWRW	GNo	5	9.6E-03	wardths5	5.7E+05	Regional nuclear war + regional SLS failure
	Global War (GWAC)	Yes	Yes	GNo	6	5.1E-02	wardths6	5.0E+05	Global conventional war + regional SLS failure
			NWGW	GNo	7	5.9E-04	wardths7	2.5E+05	Global nuclear war + regional SLS failure
		EMPAC	Yes	GNo	8	5.7E-04	wardths8	1.2E+05	Global conventional war + global SLS failure
			NWEMP	GNo	9	5.7E-04	wardths9	7.8E+05	Global nuclear war + global SLS failure
						3.03E+00		2.8E+06	Total armed conflict risk

Initiator	Scale of Conflict?	No nuclear EMP weapons used?	No other nuclear weapons used?	SLS systems maintained?	#	Frequency (events/yr)	End State	Risk (PF/yr)	Comments
biowar					1		wardths1	0.0E+00	Civil war
					2		wardths2	0.0E+00	Civil war + local SLS failure
	Regional War	GYes	GYes	Yes	3	5.5E-02	wardths3	1.7E+04	Regional conventional war
				SLSRW	4	8.4E-03	wardths4	1.0E+04	Regional conventional war + local SLS failure
			NWRW	GNo	5	5.5E-04	wardths5	3.3E+04	Regional nuclear war + regional SLS failure
	Global War (GWTW)	Yes	Yes	GNo	6	9.1E-03	wardths6	9.0E+04	Global conventional war + regional SLS failure
			NWGW	GNo	7	1.1E-04	wardths7	4.5E+04	Global nuclear war + regional SLS failure
		EMPBW	Yes	GNo	8	2.6E-04	wardths8	5.5E+04	Global conventional war + global SLS failure
			NWEMP	GNo	9	2.6E-04	wardths9	3.5E+05	Global nuclear war + global SLS failure
						7.31E-02		6.0E+05	Total bio war risk

WAR EVENT TREES

terrorwar

Event tree branches: Scale of Conflict? (Regional War, Global War (GWTW)); No nuclear EMP weapons used? (GYes, Yes, EMPTW); No other nuclear weapons used? (GYes, NWRW, Yes, NWGW, Yes, NWEMP); SLS systems maintained? (Yes, SLSRW, GNo)

#	Frequency (events/yr)	End State	Risk (PF/yr)	Comments
1		wardths1	0.0E+00	Civil war
2		wardths2	0.0E+00	Civil war + local SLS failure
3	4.0E-02	wardths3	1.2E+04	Regional conventional war
4	6.1E-03	wardths4	7.5E+03	Regional conventional war + local SLS failure
5	4.0E-04	wardths5	2.4E+04	Regional nuclear war + regional SLS failure
6	6.9E-03	wardths6	6.8E+04	Global conventional war + regional SLS failure
7	8.1E-05	wardths7	3.4E+04	Global nuclear war + regional SLS failure
8	4.1E-05	wardths8	8.7E+03	Global conventional war + global SLS failure
9	4.1E-05	wardths9	5.7E+04	Global nuclear war + global SLS failure
	5.34E-02		2.1E+05	Total terror war risk

crashwar

Event tree branches: Scale of Conflict? (Regional War, Global War (GWTW)); No nuclear EMP weapons used? (GYes, Yes, EMPCW); No other nuclear weapons used? (GYes, NWRW, Yes, NWGW, Yes, NWEMP); SLS systems maintained? (Yes, SLSRW, GNo)

#	Frequency (events/yr)	End State	Risk (PF/yr)	Comments
1		wardths1	0.0E+00	Civil war
2		wardths2	0.0E+00	Civil war + local SLS failure
3	2.5E-02	wardths3	7.7E+03	Regional conventional war
4	3.9E-03	wardths4	4.8E+03	Regional conventional war + local SLS failure
5	2.5E-04	wardths5	1.5E+04	Regional nuclear war + regional SLS failure
6	4.2E-03	wardths6	4.1E+04	Global conventional war + regional SLS failure
7	4.9E-05	wardths7	2.1E+04	Global nuclear war + regional SLS failure
8	1.2E-04	wardths8	2.5E+04	Global conventional war + global SLS failure
9	1.2E-04	wardths9	1.6E+05	Global nuclear war + global SLS failure
	3.37E-02		2.8E+05	Total crash war risk

Chapter 21 - MFRA REFERENCES

The following references are called out in Part IV, the MFRA risk model, or provide good background for the following subjects.

Kinetic Impact Events
1. Earth Impact Effects Program, Collins, Melosh, and Marcus, *Meteoritics & Planetary Science* 40, Nr 6, 817–840 (2005)
2. Impact Event, *Wikipedia*, 7/20/2014
3. Population Agglomerations of the World, Thomas Brinkhoff: City Population, *http://www.citypopulation.de*

Natural Terrestrial Events
4. Supervolcano, *Wikipedia*, 7/20/2014
5. Volcano Hazards Program, U.S. Geological Survey, http://volcanoes.usgs.gov/
6. Earthquake Hazards Program, U.S. Geological Survey, http://earthquake.usgs.gov/
7. List of Deadliest Floods, *Wikipedia*, 7/20/2014
8. List of Famines, *Wikipedia*, 9/4/2014
9. Food riots predicted over US crop failure, Robert Kennedy, *Al Jazeera*, 8/21/2012
10. Magnetic Pole Reversal Happens All The (Geologic) Time, NASA.gov

Electric Power Failure Risks
11. Solar Storm Threat Analysis, James A. Marusek, *Impact 2007*
12. Solar Storm Risk to the North American Electric Grid, Lloyd's 2013
13. Near Miss: The Solar Superstorm of July 2012, Phillips, Tony, *NASA Science News*, 7/23/2013
14. Severe Space Weather--Social and Economic Impacts, Phillips, Tony, *NASA Science News*, 1/21/2009
15. Severe Space Weather Events—Understanding Societal and Economic Impacts Workshop Report, National Research Council, 2008

16. Report of the Commission to Assess the Threat to the United States from Electromagnetic Pulse (EMP) Attack, Graham, et al, 2004

17. Report of the Commission to Assess the Threat to the United States from Electromagnetic Pulse (EMP) Attack, Graham, et al, 2008

18. Failure to Protect U.S. Against Electromagnetic Pulse Threat Could Make 9/11 Look Trivial Someday, Kelly-Detwiler, Peter, *Forbes*, 7/31/2014

19. The Growing Threat From an EMP Attack, R. James Woolsey & Peter Vincent Pry, *The Wall Street Journal*, 8/13/2014

20. Assault on California Power Station Raises Alarm on Potential for Terrorism, Rebecca Smith, *The Wall Street Journal*, 2/5/2014

21. America's Power Is Under Threat, Peggy Noonan, *The Wall Street Journal*, 2/7/2014

22. U.S. Risks National Blackout From Small-Scale Attack, Rebecca Smith, *The Wall Street Journal*, 3/12/2014

23. DOE: Information on Power Grid Threats Should Have Been Classified, Rebecca Smith, *The Wall Street Journal*, 4/9/2014

24. Federal Government Is Urged to Prevent Grid Attacks, Rebecca Smith, *The Wall Street Journal*, 7/7/2014

25. Power Station's Security Is Breached, Again, Rebecca Smith, *The Wall Street Journal*, 8/29/2014

Biological Risks
26. List of epidemics, *Wikipedia*, 7/20/2014

27. Pandemic Severity Index, Centers for Disease Control and Prevention, http://www.cdc.gov/media/pdf/MitigationSlides.pdf

28. Influenza Pandemic Periodicity, Virus Recycling, and the Art of Risk Assessment, Walter R. Dowdle, *Emerging Infectious Diseases*, Vol. 12, No. 1, January 2006

29. The Laboratory Response Network, Centers for Disease Control and Prevention, http://emergency.cdc.gov/lrn/pdf/lrn-overview-presentation.pdf

30. Ebola's Warning for an Unprepared America, *The Wall Street Journal*, 9/17/2014
31. BSL-4 Laboratories as of 2010-2011, Federation of American Scientists, https://www.google.com/fusiontables/DataSource?sna pid=S567513UnBn
32. Day of synthetic pathogens-based bioterrorism nears, *Homeland Security Newsletter*, 9/16/2010
33. Experiments with dangerous bird flu stains pose risk of accidental release, *Homeland Security Newsletter*, 5/27/2014
34. Nearly 400 Accidents with Dangerous Pathogens and Biotoxins Reported in U.S. Labs over 7 Years, Katherine Harmon Courage, *Scientific American*, 10/3/2011
35. CDC scientist took shortcuts handling deadly bird flu virus, investigation finds, Lena H. Sun and Brady Dennis, *The Washington Post*, 8/15/2014
36. More deadly pathogens, toxins found improperly stored in NIH and FDA labs, Lena H. Sun and Brady Dennis, *The Washington Post*, 9/5/2014
37. How secure are labs handling world's deadliest pathogens?, Sharon Begley and Julie Steenhuysen, *Reuters*, 2/15/2012
38. Ebola is 'devouring everything in its path.' Could it lead to Liberia's collapse?, Abby Ohlheiser, *The Washington Post*, 9/12/2014
39. Anthrax Scare at CDC Labs, Betsy McKay, *The Wall Street Journal*, 6/20/2014
40. Accidents Prompt CDC to Halt Lab Sample Shipments, *The Wall Street Journal*, 7/12/2014
41. CDC Lab Head resigns After Anthrax Incident, *The Wall Street Journal*, 7/24/2014
42. *The Demon in the Freezer*, Richard Preston, Random House, 2012

Economic & Financial Risks
43. Financial and Sovereign Debt Crises: Some Lessons Learned and Those Forgotten, Carmen M. Reinhart and

Kenneth S. Rogoff, *International Monetary Fund*, WP/13/266, December 2013
44. Financial Repression Redux, Carmen M. Reinhart, Jacob F. Kirkegaard, and M. Belen Sbrancia, *Finance & Development*, June 2011
45. *A New-Old Way to Get Out From Under*, Stephen Fidler, *The Wall Street Journal*, 7/12/2013
46. Obstacle to Deficit Cutting: A Nation on Entitlements, Sara Murray, *The Wall Street Journal*, 9/15/2010
47. List of economic crises, *Wikipedia*, 7/20/2014
48. The Government Bond Racket, *The Wall Street Journal*, Editorial, 7/14/2014
49. Stop Us Before We Kill Again, *The Wall Street Journal*, Editorial, 7/1/2014
50. Banking Business: Complexity Cubed, Dan Fitzpatrick & Michael R. Crittenden, *The Wall Street Journal*, 4/11/2013
51. The Magnitude of the Mess We're In, George P. Schultz, et al, *The Wall Street Journal*, 9/17/2012

War
53. List of wars 1945–1989, *Wikipedia*, 7/16/2014
54. List of wars 1990–2002, *Wikipedia*, 7/16/2014
55. *The Better Angels of Our Nature*, Steven Pinker, Viking Penguin, 2011
56. Power Failure, Robert Kagan, *The Wall Street Journal*, 9/6/2014
57. In Fight for Syria, Food and Medicine Are Weapons of War, *The Wall Street Journal*, 1/21/2014
58. Asian Nations Fear War with China, *The Wall Street Journal*, 7/15/2014
59. The Growing Threat From an EMP Attack, R. James Woolsey & Peter Vincent Pry, *The Wall Street Journal*, 8/13/2014
60. *The World America Made*, Robert Kagan, Alfred A. Knopf, 2012, ISBN 978-0-307-96131-0

Part V – Revisiting the Report Card on Risk Management

Let's take a look back now at the events and ideas we have covered in this book. I hope that you will find these final comments to be especially meaningful because now we can communicate using the full lexicon of the language of risk management.

In Part I we began with a review of the horrific Macondo oil well blowout. In reading the accident investigation reports it quickly became apparent that the BP team was a victim of their own risk compliant attitude. I think they really believed that the drilling operation was safe because it complied with existing regulations that required the installation of a blowout preventer (BOP). As a result, no Macondo specific assessment of blowout risk was made. This accident illustrates how dangerous such an attitude can be. A risk proactive organization would make their own independent assessment of risk and put the regulations on trial. They would ask: Are the government regulations good enough for us?

Next we examined the soft underbelly of the Great Recession and found wildly risk prone behavior. Claims of rigorous risk management practices were founded on malicious assumptions that ignored dependencies between financial instruments and among financial institutions, and these practices were callously used to hide extreme risk taking. We also saw how both the financial industry and its regulators failed to appreciate how suddenly and completely a complex dynamic system can collapse.

The saddest of our three case studies had to be the Tōhoku – Fukushima tragedy. The Tōhoku earthquake was obviously a violent act of God. Although many lives were lost, Japanese preparations, including an early warning system, worked to no doubt save many lives. These sound preparations did not extend, however, to the Fukushima Daiichi reactors.

Even though it is now more than three years since the Fukushima Daiichi meltdowns, a comprehensive understanding of why earthquake and tsunami risk was so badly managed for this power plant has yet to emerge. Even though Tepco officials have now admitted their culpability in the inadequate plant design, just blaming current officials doesn't explain the bad decisions made over decades. Questions remaining to be answered include:

- Why wasn't evidence of the 869 AD earthquake and tsunami used in setting the original design bases for the plant?
- How were units 1-4 allowed to continue operating without meaningful upgrades after units 5 & 6 were built to higher standards?
- Why were additional emergency generators installed without reliable connections to the units 1-4 emergency core cooling systems?

We may never know.

In Chapter 5 I examined the status of professionalism in risk management and concluded that it is not yet recognized as an independent profession. Because of this, risk management is too often left to subject matter experts (SME's) to perform as best they can, with predictably inconsistent outcomes. I further concluded that the management of risk will not advance to the higher level I believe is needed until high hazard activities like those reviewed in our case studies are required to undergo review by independent risk management professionals. But this is not likely to happen because I say so. What I can accomplish though is to equip the reader with the knowledge he or she needs to ascertain whether or not risk is being managed well in areas important to them. This was the objective of Parts II and III.

Part II began with an overview of the basic process of managing risk. In this process three major tasks were highlighted; performing risk assessments, understanding risk assessment results, and identifying and implementing risk reduction actions. The basic methods and tools needed to perform risk assessments were described in Chapter 7. The application of these risk assessment methods requires a basic knowledge of the use of probability distributions. Because this is an important subject and one that can intimidate some and scare them away from using risk analysis, I laid out what I hope is a useful guide to this subject that everyone can understand in Chapter 8. Chapter 9 concluded the basic how to section with a discussion of what quantitative risk assessment results look like and how to use them to set appropriate goals or limits and also how to use the results to identify available risk reduction actions.

With our risk management tool kit now in hand, we began to practice what we preached. In Part III I used a risk management tool introduced in Part II, the master logic diagram, to organize the discussion of ways that risk management can fail. In Chapter 11 I pulled back the curtain on some of the creative excuses I have seen used for ignoring risk. I hope you were both entertained and disturbed by reading Chapter 11 because actively ignoring risk is one the major causes of catastrophes like the ones we reviewed in Part I. Chapter 12 turned up the microscope on the leading reasons why risk assessments can sometimes produce bad results and lead people making a sincere effort to manage risk down the wrong path. This was the place I chose to deal with two of the most conceptually difficult topics included in this book. The first topic was the proper assessment of evidence in the determination of uncertainty. Although Bayes Theorem provides the cornerstone for understanding this problem, its direct application can be difficult and I introduced a practical alternative called Risk Factor Analysis. Dependence, both the most difficult and most important problem to master in conducting risk assessments was the second topic. Here I described the different types of dependencies that need to be addressed and then described the ways these dependencies can be modeled. I conclude the discussion of dependence by describing the indicators you should look for to tell if a risk analysis has done a good job on this issue. Next, I examined the reasons why clearly identified risks sometimes go unaddressed and are allowed to unnecessarily cause failure. Here I introduced a spectrum of risk management maturity levels to help to understand and categorize risk taking behavior in individuals or organizations. To complete Part III, I recast the key points from all of Part III into a forward looking set of questions that can be used by anyone as a checklist to perform a risk management review for any subject or activity of concern.

To complete our journey through the world of risk management, I wanted to put my preaching to the test and actually demonstrate how to assess and manage risk with a real world example. To do this I needed a subject that was both doable and of interest to a broad audience. One idea I came up with was to look at the risk for a potentially catastrophic natural event like an asteroid strike. That would be something with broad interest (many SyFy movies) and I thought I would be able to find applicable data. When I began to look for data that I might be able to work with I also became curious about just how important asteroid strikes might be compared to other possible calamities. It surprised me when I found no such benchmark in the available literature. There are many who have conjectured in qualitative terms about how bad it would be if this or that terrible event actually happened, but I found no concise quantitative analysis of existential risk. So I thought; well......., let's take a shot at the big picture. The result is now Part IV of this book.

In retrospect taking on the broader topic of what I came to call mega fatality risk was maybe a bit too big a bite, but it was definitely fun to do. I think it worked beyond my expectations, however, as example of how quantitative risk analysis can be used to move an individual or an organization from one state of knowledge (none) to a much higher level, enabling risk informed decisions and performance improving investments to be made.

So in closing, let me just restate some of the important things I learned from performing this exercise.

- Mankind has suffered some pretty awful calamities in our history, but none in recorded history have come even close to threatening our continued existence.

- Because of our current large population (7.2 billion) examining only events that would wipe us all out could miss really important threats that fall between what we have actually experienced and extinction.

- Loss of an electric power system over a large area for any significant duration could place the survival of millions in jeopardy. The MFRA identified multiple events that could cause this to happen at relatively high frequencies. This made loss of electric power as a risk category comparable with pandemics and war in the total mega fatality risk profile.

- In light of the previous finding, comprehensive research on the dynamics of events like the extended loss of electric power should be conducted to develop meaningful risk reduction strategies.

- Although the ability to perform medical research with pathogens is obviously necessary, the maintenance of deadly special agents in forty or more BSL-4 labs, some of which are in high population areas and/or high natural phenomena risk areas, presents a significant risk for accidental or deliberate releases.

- The only act of God event found to contribute significantly to mega fatality risk was solar storms.

If you have comments or questions you would like to ask about mega fatality risk, or any other part of the book, please visit my website at *jpkindinger.com* and let me know what you think.

Acknowledgements

I owe a great deal of thanks to the many people who helped me gain the knowledge and the confidence to undertake this project. Among the most important in this group were Dr. B John Garrick, Dr. Stan Kaplan, Karl Fleming, Dr. Frank Hubbard, and Dr. Andy Dykes from my years at PLG. The list of important contributors from LANL is too long to list but special thanks must go to Dr. Desmond Stack who gave me opportunity to be a member of that special family and to Bonnie Koch who repeatedly encouraged me to write down my lessons learned so that others might be able to benefit.

In the actual production of this book, the most important supporters were my wife Cindy whose patience and editorial expertise were invaluable and Dr. Andy Dykes who helped provide a technical peer review.

Now I'm ready for the next project!

Risk Management Glossary

Aleatory uncertainty.- Aleatory uncertainty is the inherent randomness that remains after all relevant and available knowledge about an event or condition has been discovered.

Conditional probability – The likelihood that an event in a scenario occurs, or not, conditioned on all the events that precede it in the scenario.

Consequence analysis – Assesses the resulting damage or loss that would be realized for each scenario, given that it occurs. The results of the risk analysis are then obtained by summing all the conditional damages by the frequencies of the corresponding scenarios.

Consequence measures – Metrics defined to measure injury or loss incurred from a risk scenario. Examples include human deaths and monetary loss.

Continuous distribution – A probability distribution where a random variable can take on any value between the specified low and high limits.

Defense in depth – A risk management strategy that employs redundant and diverse risk reduction actions to address hazards.

Discrete distribution – A probability distribution where the variable under study can only take on certain specific values (e.g. heads or tails).

Dynamic simulation – A mathematical modeling tool that predicts the behavior of a defined system as a function of time.

Epistemic uncertainty - Epistemic uncertainty is the uncertainty arising from imperfect knowledge about the event or condition in question.

Event tree – An inductive logic modeling tool that charts the progression of a scenario from an initiating event through conditional top events to an end state.

Event tree end state – A stable condition realized at the conclusion of a risk scenario.

Event tree initiating event – The first event in a scenario.

Event tree scenario – A predicted series of events leading from an initiating event to a measurable end state. A risk analysis includes a description of the "as planned" scenario which generally defines success for the planned endeavor as well as failure scenarios which end in various degrees of injury, loss, or damage.

Event tree split fraction – The conditional probability assigned to a branch point in an event tree.

Event tree top event – Questions listed on the top of an event tree that describe conditional events that may or may not occur to define a scenario.

Fault tree – A deductive logic modeling tool that illustrates the logical paths from elementary basic events to a specified top event.

Frequency – The quantitative result of an experiment involving repeated trials. Frequency can be expressed as the number of events observed in a measured number of trials (N/T) or as the number of events observed per unit of time (e.g. deaths per year).

Hazard – An inherent physical characteristic that has the potential for causing harm to people, property, or the environment.

Likelihood – The chance that something will happen

Likelihood analysis – Determines the resulting frequency of each possible scenario from the Scenario Analysis. The sum of all the scenario frequencies must equal the initiating event frequency.

Master logic diagram - A deductive logic modeling tool that illustrates all possible logical paths through which scenarios must pass to produce a specified top event.

Monte Carlo simulation – A calculation performed repeatedly with parameter values selected randomly from probability distributions.

Probability – The science of determining likelihood from limited or no frequency type data. Probability is the numerical expression of a state of knowledge or confidence.

Qualitative risk assessment – A risk analysis performed using methods that rank the likelihood and consequence of risk scenarios in a relative sense: that is relative to each other (more, about the same, less) and/or a qualitative ranking scale (e.g. high, medium, low).

Quantitative risk assessment – A risk analysis performed using methods that express the likelihood and consequences of risk scenarios on absolute numeric scales.

Risk – The chance of injury, loss, or damage resulting from exposure to a hazard. Expressed symbolically, Risk = Hazard/Safeguards. Risk can also be thought of as uncertainty that matters. An example of the difference between risk and uncertainty is illustrated by an inheritance of an unknown amount. The recipient of the inheritance may have great uncertainty about how much he or she will receive, but there is no risk.

Risk assessment/analysis – The science of predicting future conditions considering the possible success or failure of planned actions in the presence of hazards.

Risk curve – A graphic plot describing the assessed range of possible frequency and consequence results for a risk scenario or category of scenarios.

Risk management – The science of using risk analysis to make informed decisions with imperfect knowledge.

Risk matrix – A graphic arrangement of rows and columns where categories of likelihood and consequence are used to rank potential risk events or issues.

Risk watch list – A ranked list of assessed risk issues complete with recommended risk reduction actions.

Safeguards – Protective or mitigative measures reducing the chance of injury, loss, or damage resulting from exposure to a hazard

Statistics – The science of determining likelihood from available frequency type data

System - An entity comprised of interacting discrete elements functioning to achieve some beneficial objective.

Uncertainty analysis – An assessment of the confidence with which the likelihood analysis and consequence analysis questions can be answered, this is expressed in terms of probability.

Index

About the Author

John P. Kindinger is an author and semi-retired engineer living in Eustis, Florida. Before moving to Florida, John was employed at the Los Alamos National Laboratory where he served as Nuclear Design and Risk Analysis Group Leader. Prior to joining LANL, John was Manager of Risk Assessment Technology at ARES Corporation and a senior consultant with Pickard, Lowe, & Garrick (PLG), Inc. in Newport Beach, CA. Before that, he was employed as a staff engineer for the Consumers Power Company in Jackson, Michigan.

John has extensive experience in the assessment of risk for complex projects and important investment decisions and safety analysis for defense nuclear facilities, nuclear power plants, and other high hazard facilities. He holds a BS in Mechanical Engineering from Michigan State University and a MS in the Management of Technology from the Massachusetts Institute of Technology.

Follow John's activities at jpkindinger.com.

www.ingramcontent.com/pod-product-compliance
Lightning Source LLC
Chambersburg PA
CBHW060014210326
41520CB00009B/886